Dag Hammarskjold

PEACEMAKER FOR THE U.N.

The Yin and the Yang, *an ancient Chinese figure, is symbolic for Century Books, since both negative and positive forces which the figure represents also shape the lives of famous world figures.*

According to folklore, the Yin and the Yang are present in all things, functioning together in perpetual interaction. This balance between opposing forces, and the influences, both good and bad, that have molded the course of history are accurately portrayed as background material in Century biographies.

Dag Hammarskjold

PEACEMAKER FOR THE U.N.

by Elizabeth Rider Montgomery

A CENTURY BOOK

GARRARD PUBLISHING COMPANY
CHAMPAIGN, ILLINOIS

For Deborah Small

Acknowledgments:

The excerpts on pages 73, 75, 87, 88, 100, 120, 121, 143–144, 146–147, and 159 are reprinted from *Dag Hammarskjold: Servant of Peace*, edited by Wilder Foote, published by Harper and Row, Publishers, Inc., 1962.

The excerpts on pages 17, 33, 34, 35, 37, 51–52, 63, 68, 69, 70, 71, 78, 86, 99, 100, 106, 114, 121, 151, 152, 155, and 168 are reprinted from *Markings*, by Dag Hammarskjold, translated by Leif Sjoberg and W. H. Auden. Copyright © 1964 by Alfred A. Knopf, Inc., and Faber and Faber, Ltd. Reprinted by permission of Alfred A. Knopf, Inc.

Picture credits on page 176

Library of Congress Cataloging in Publication Data

Montgomery, Elizabeth Rider.
    Dag Hammarskjold: Peacemaker for the UN

    (A Century book)
    SUMMARY: A biography of the second Secretary-General of the United Nations who died in a plane crash on a peace mission to the Congo in 1961.

    1. Hammarskjold, Dag, 1905–1961—Juvenile literature.
[1. Hammarskjold, Dag, 1905–1961. 2. United Nations—Bibliography] I. Title.
D839.7.H3M65   341.23′2 [B] [92]   73–570
ISBN 0–8116–4757–9

Contents

1. "I Would Be Crazy to Accept"

On an afternoon in March 1953, Dag Hammarskjold, one of Sweden's top career diplomats, kept an appointment for a portrait sitting in a Stockholm studio. The directors of the Bank of Sweden had commissioned Bo Beskow to paint Hammarskjold's portrait. Dag Hammarskjold had served the bank faithfully for many years, while holding other government posts at the same time. This would be the first portrait sitting.

When Hammarskjold was seated in the studio, the artist looked at his subject thoughtfully. He saw a tall, slim, clean-cut man with blue eyes, sandy hair, and a high forehead. Hammarskjold was nice looking, but he would not stand out in a crowd.

Beskow found the forty-eight-year-old Hammarskjold a challenging subject to paint. He kept a pose perfectly, unmoving and unchanging. He was completely cool and self-disciplined, never allowing himself to relax.

The artist, however, liked his models to forget he was painting them. In order to take Hammarskjold's mind off of the portrait, Beskow began to ask questions as he sketched.

Courteously and clearly, Dag Hammarskjold responded to queries about art, music, theater, poetry, philosophy, and politics. The breadth and depth of Hammarskjold's knowledge and the soundness of his judgment amazed Beskow. Usually the artist scarcely listened as his models replied to his questions, but today he grew so interested in the conversation that he almost forgot his work. Dag, on the other hand, always remembered to keep his disciplined pose.

In succeeding weeks the sittings continued, and so did the conversations. Beskow heard fascinating discussions on a variety of subjects, often—after the first day —volunteered by Dag. Hammarskjold talked about the flora and fauna of Lapland, where he had hiked and camped since his student days at the University of Uppsala. He described the techniques of mountain climbing, his favorite sport. He related the history of famous churches, cathedrals, and castles, including the cathedral at Uppsala, which he had attended throughout his childhood and youth.

Beskow knew, as did all of Sweden, that Dag's father, Hjalmar Hammarskjold, had spent his life in the service of his country as statesman and diplomat. The senior Hammarskjold had always insisted on Sweden's neutrality and constantly tried to promote world peace.

Dag had followed in his father's footsteps. When

only twenty-five, he had gone into government work and had since held various positions in Sweden's Finance and Foreign Ministries. He had served on important diplomatic commissions, such as the history-making Organization for European Economic Cooperation after World War II. He was presently Sweden's vice-minister of foreign affairs.

Dag had continued his father's work toward peace, but there was a vast difference in the methods of father and son. During the senior Hammarskjold's days of power, he had antagonized many people by his autocratic ways. Dag, on the other hand, was skilled at winning the cooperation of those with whom he dealt. As a diplomat and a peacemaker, Dag Hammarskjold had no peer. He was often called on to mediate quarrels and negotiate compromises at various levels of government. Beskow had heard many reports of Dag's talent for peacemaking.

One afternoon Beskow, who shared his model's interest in world affairs, brought up the subject of the United Nations. Only recently Dag had returned from New York City, where he had gone as a member of the Swedish delegation to the United Nations. While there, he had heard much speculation about a new secretary-general.

Trygve Lie of Norway had been secretary-general of the United Nations since its founding. Lie had found the office a heavy burden as it was impossible to please everyone. When Lie supported Russia in any controversy, the Western powers were indignant. When he approved an American or Western European stand, his action angered the Soviet Union. For the past year he had been under pressure from the Soviets to resign.

"Loyalty investigations" by the United States government of Americans on the United Nations staff added to Lie's difficulties. When he tried to take a stand against the FBI's fingerprinting of these employees, he did not receive the support he expected from other nations. Instead, he was criticized from all sides. In November 1952, Trygve Lie announced that he had decided "after lengthy consideration" to resign his position. His resignation was to take effect as soon as a replacement could be found.

By the terms of the United Nations Charter, the secretary-general is appointed by the General Assembly on the recommendation of the Security Council. The secretary-general acts as a spokesman for the UN, and actually is a symbol of the organization throughout the world. The United Nations' secretary-general has a very important post—perhaps the most important in the world.

At the time Dag was in New York, the Security Council was finding it difficult to agree on a replacement for Trygve Lie. The Soviet Union would not accept a secretary-general from one of the great Western powers. That ruled out the United States, England, and France. Western nations would not consider a candidate from any member of the Iron Curtain group. That ruled out the Soviet Union and all her satellites, such as Hungary, Rumania, Bulgaria, and Czechoslovakia. Candidates from Poland, Canada, the Philippines, India, and several other nations were rejected for one reason or another.

The ideal secretary-general of the United Nations must be free from any political entanglements. He must have no ties whatever with either the Soviet bloc of nations or the Western bloc. He needs to be an experienced statesman and a masterly diplomat, trained in law and economics. The office requires a high order of intelligence, great resourcefulness, and superhuman physical endurance.

As Beskow painted and Dag Hammarskjold held to his disciplined pose, the two men discussed possible candidates for secretary-general. None who was suggested seemed good enough.

Suddenly the artist laid down his brush. He looked at his model as if he had never seen him before.

"Do you know," he exclaimed, "*you* would make a good secretary-general!"

Dag smiled. "Nobody is crazy enough to propose me," he replied. "And I would be crazy to accept."

On the other side of the Atlantic Ocean, several other men had the same idea as Bo Beskow. One of them was Henri Hoppenot, a representative from France who had worked with Dag on the Organization for European Economic Cooperation (OEEC). He suggested Dag's name to Henry Cabot Lodge, United States' ambassador to the UN, who was active in the search for a new secretary-general.

"Dag Hammarskjold?" Lodge repeated. "Who is he?"

Hoppenot related what he knew of Dag's meteoric career. Hammarskjold came from an aristocratic Swedish family, which had a long, proud tradition of public service. His education had been exceptional; his reputation was spotless; and his talent for diplomacy was unquestioned. Currently he was being mentioned as a possibility for prime minister of Sweden. He had been proposed as chancellor of the Swedish universities, for important ambassadorial posts, and as lord lieutenant of a province. Few men in Sweden stood higher in their countrymen's esteem than Dag Hammarskjold.

Lodge agreed that Hammarskjold's qualifications for the post of secretary-general seemed impressive. Besides, he was a Swede, and Sweden's traditional neutrality would help his candidacy.

Lodge sounded out the other delegations about Dag Hammarskjold. He soon learned that several

Americans had seen Dag in action in 1946, when the Swedish-American trade agreements had been renegotiated. Delegates from many other nations had—like Hoppenot—observed his work on the OEEC. All had been impressed with Hammarskjold's capabilities.

Lodge was instructed by his government in Washington, D.C.: "If you can get Hammarskjold, grab him."

On March 31, at a meeting of the eleven-member Security Council, Hoppenot formally nominated Dag Hammarskjold for the post of UN's secretary-general. The British delegate seconded the nomination, and Dag's name was approved. It only remained for the General Assembly, composed of representatives of sixty nations, to ratify the nomination.

In Stockholm, in the middle of the night on March 31, Dag Hammarskjold's telephone began to ring. A newspaper reporter was on the line. He said that the wire service had just received a report that Hammarskjold had been nominated by the Security Council for secretary-general of the UN. What was his reaction?

Dag had heard nothing whatever about the recent United Nations' discussions. He had no inkling that his name had been under consideration for any post. He replied shortly that the report was merely rumor. Then he hung up the phone and went back to bed.

A few minutes later his telephone rang again. This time a friend, who was a newspaper editor, was on the line. He had seen the same wire service report. Although Dag was usually even-tempered and extremely courteous, he spoke irritably to his friend.

"I haven't heard a word about it. I might have understood if this had been tomorrow (April Fools' Day), but even then I would have considered it as a cruel joke."

However, an official message soon arrived from the president of the UN Security Council, and Dag knew that he had indeed been proposed for the post of secretary-general. Should he, or should he not, accept the formidable responsibility?

As was his custom when facing an important decision, Dag took the matter up with his father. A tall, thin, bald-headed man of unfailing dignity, Hjalmar Hammarskjold was now ninety-one years of age. He was in failing health, but his mind remained alert and keen.

Hjalmar Hammarskjold had spent more than fifty years in the service of his country. He had served Sweden as minister of justice, minister of education, president of a high court, ambassador to Denmark, lord lieutenant (governor) of Uppland Province, and prime minister. He had also been a key member of various diplomatic missions. It seemed that whenever a touchy situation arose in Swedish foreign policy,

Hjalmar Hammarskjold—
devoted public servant,
trusted adviser, and a
man of firm convictions

Hjalmar Hammarskjold was usually asked to be one of the negotiators. He had brought up his four sons to believe that no career was as satisfying as that of a government servant.

When Dag asked his advice concerning the secretary-general nomination, old Mr. Hammarskjold needed no time to consider his reply.

"Take it," he replied crisply. "Your whole life has been pointed toward this day."

His father's words expressed Dag's own secret

thoughts. The post of United Nations' secretary-general would provide a tremendous challenge. It would offer a chance to do useful, important work—work for world peace. He might, as he had observed to Beskow, be crazy to accept the job, but accept he would.

Dag telephoned his superior in the Swedish Foreign Ministry and asked to be released from his cabinet position. Then he cabled the UN Security Council that he would accept the nomination.

Dag had a one o'clock appointment for a portrait sitting at Bo Beskow's studio. As usual, he arrived promptly.

Beskow had seen the headlines splashed across the morning newspapers: "DAG HAMMARSKJOLD NEW SECRETARY-GENERAL OF THE UNITED NATIONS?" He asked his model eagerly, "Did you accept?"

"Yes," Dag replied. "I must take it, difficult though it is. It is my duty." Dag seemed pleased and excited.

"Could you sleep at all last night?" Beskow inquired.

"Yes, of course," Dag answered. "Why shouldn't I sleep?"

"Well, if this had happened to me, I wouldn't have slept a wink," Beskow said. "Or else I would have had terrible nightmares."

"I never have dreams like that," Dag responded with a smile. "I have tried to do my job, and I have always slept well."

Little was accomplished on the painting that afternoon. The two men, who had become firm friends by now, talked on and on about the new position.

Since Dag Hammarskjold never revealed his deep spiritual beliefs, he did not tell Beskow that for several years he had been praying for guidance concerning his career. He had been trying to find the "right road," the path that would enable him to do the greatest good for mankind.

That night he wrote in his secret journal:

Your prayer has been answered, as you know.
God has a use for you . . .

2. Son of Sweden's Leader

At the time of Dag's birth, on July 29, 1905, in Jonkoping, Sweden, his father, Hjalmar Hammarskjold, was in Norway. He was a member of a commission to dissolve the centuries-old union between Norway and Sweden. The negotiations dragged on and on, and almost four months passed before the matter was settled and Mr. Hammarskjold returned home. At last Dag could be properly christened.

For the next two years the family lived in Denmark, while Mr. Hammarskjold served as Sweden's ambassador to that country. Then Hjalmar Hammarskjold was named lord lieutenant of Uppland Province, and the Hammarskjolds moved to the university town of Uppsala, Sweden.

Uppsala Castle was the only home that Dag remembered from his childhood. The 400-year-old castle was the official home of the lord lieutenant of the province. In earlier centuries it had been the residence of Swedish kings. With eight-foot-thick walls, uneven stone floors, and deeply recessed tiny windows, the castle was a fascinating place for a small boy to live. It had numerous towers, turrets, and battlements. There were winding underground passages, mysterious unused rooms, and cold, scary dungeons. Dag loved to take guests on tours of exploration.

The Hammarskjold family lived in one wing of the huge, dark castle, while another wing held the government offices. On state occasions some of the grand tower rooms were opened, especially the circular banquet room.

The castle grounds with park-like woods and beautiful gardens were as interesting as the castle itself. One garden, nationally famous, had flowers and shrubs from all parts of Sweden. Each one was tagged with its proper botanical name.

From the time he was quite small, Dag loved this garden. He memorized the names of the plants and collected specimens of each one. He liked to lie on the ground in the woods and watch the birds that flew from branch to branch over his head, and the insects that crawled on the forest floor. By the time he was ten, he had learned to identify almost all of the birds, insects, and flowers of Uppland Province.

Partly from necessity and partly from choice, Dag spent a great deal of time alone. His three brothers were quite a lot older than he. Bo, fourteen years his senior, and Ake, twelve years older, had both followed the Hammarskjold family tradition and gone into government service. Dag's third brother, Sten, was only

Dag's childhood home was Uppsala Castle, the residence of the lord lieutenant of Uppland Province.

five years older than he, but that was enough to keep the two youngest Hammarskjold boys from being close companions. Sometimes Dag played with the children of Archbishop Soderblom. They lived in the Archiepiscopal Palace across from the cathedral at the bottom of the hill. However, Dag was naturally shy and reserved, and he seldom sought out companions.

In May 1914, the king of Sweden asked Hjalmar Hammarskjold to be his prime minister. For the next three years Stockholm was Hammarskjold's headquarters, although he still held his post as lord lieutenant of Uppland Province.

Unlike her stern and formal husband, Agnes Hammarskjold fairly bubbled with good humor and affection. She was a beautiful woman, with sparkling brown eyes and dark hair. Plump, lively, and cheerful, she charmed everyone she met. Since she came from a family of teachers, preachers, philosophers, and poets, it was natural for her to be interested in music, art, and literature.

One of Mrs. Hammarskjold's most endearing traits was her concern for the welfare of others. She was continually taking food to hungry families, finding work for idle workmen, and cheering those who grieved. The whole countryside depended on Mrs. Hammarskjold for help in emergencies, and everybody loved her. Dag adored her.

Hjalmar Hammarskjold's years of service as prime minister of Sweden made a deep impression on Dag. Young as he was, he saw that his mother's life was made difficult by his father's long absences. Mrs. Hammarskjold had the responsibility for running the large household and managing the estate, as well as guiding the upbringing of her sons. Yet she never complained.

Besides creating problems for his mother, his father's post of prime minister made life miserable for Dag himself at times.

The Great War, now known as World War I, had

broken out in August of 1914 when Dag was nine. Most of the nations of Europe were involved in the conflict, but Sweden, under Mr. Hammarskjold's strong leadership, remained neutral. Great pressure was put on Prime Minister Hammarskjold to lead Sweden into the war. Germany wanted Sweden to fight at her side, and the Allies hoped to persuade her to join them. Some Swedes sympathized with Germany. Others favored the Allies.

When Prime Minister Hammarskjold insisted that Sweden must honor her trade agreements with Germany, he was charged with being pro-German. When he made his country observe commercial treaties with England and France, he was accused of helping the Allies. Nothing he did was popular.

This war was the first one in history to be fought in the air and underwater, as well as on the surface of land and sea. Not only did soldiers die in battle, but many civilians were killed by bombs dropped from airplanes. Neutral nations like Sweden lost many cargo ships to submarine warfare. Food became scarce in Sweden, and Hammarskjold was blamed. He was called "Prime Minister Hungerskjold."

His father's unpopularity affected Dag strongly. At school he was teased and tormented because many classmates' parents opposed his father's political policies. Dag often stood, alone and lonely, at one side of the school playground, knowing he was not welcome to join the other boys' games.

However, unpopularity, opposition, and hatred could not shake the prime minister's conviction that Sweden should stay out of the war. He believed firmly that war solves nothing, but creates new problems.

In 1917 Hjalmar Hammarskjold resigned as prime minister and returned to Uppsala as lord lieutenant of the province.

By this time Dag was twelve and growing tall. His features and expression strongly resembled his mother's, but his build and coloring were like his blond father's. Dag was much stronger than his lean frame would indicate, and he had a quick, keen mind.

He had a remarkable memory too. He did his schoolwork quickly and well. He also memorized quantities of poetry. He devoured books on wildlife and Swedish history and geography, meanwhile pursuing his hobbies of collecting plants and insects.

Dag often went with his mother to concerts, art exhibits, and lectures. He also accompanied her to church each Sunday and listened attentively to the sermons of Archbishop Soderblom. Afterward he waited cheerfully while his mother talked with the friends she met in the town. These were people from all walks of life—aristocrats, peasants, and the archbishop himself, who was a close friend of hers.

Twelve-year-old Dag Hammarskjold posed for this picture with his mother in 1917.

Archbishop Nathan Soderblom, head of the Swedish Lutheran Church, was a man of amazing vision and tremendous energy. Under his influence Sweden was taking the lead in the new movement to persuade all Protestant churches to work together for common goals. In later years the World Council of Churches would evolve from this work.

The Soderblom and Hammarskjold families were life-long friends as well as neighbors, and visited each other frequently. Dag admired Archbishop Soderblom greatly and found him much easier to talk to than his stern, rather formidable father.

Jon Soderblom was about Dag's own age, and the two boys attended the same school. They were also frequent companions in various sports—swimming, hiking, and camping in summer, skating and skiing in winter.

Dag belonged to a bicycle club, organized for weekend trips into the countryside. During the long days of summer, the boys would ride until late in the evening. Sometimes they camped out and returned home the following day.

Dag was a tireless hiker and a strong bicyclist. He had an inborn sense of direction. The other boys often said that when Dag Hammarskjold was with them, they did not need a map or a compass.

Dag also liked to ski. He was not outstanding at

downhill skiing, but he excelled when it came to climbing uphill. He always reached the top of a rise before the others and stood waiting for them with a cheerful smile.

Beauty of all kinds affected Dag deeply: a perfect poem, lovely music, a fine painting, a beautiful sunset, or a delicate flower. Yet his interests were not restricted to these things. He shared his mother's concern for less fortunate people, and like his father he had a natural interest in national and international affairs.

Now that Hjalmar Hammarskjold had come home to stay, he began to hold serious discussions at the dinner table with his youngest sons. He had followed this practice when his oldest boys, Bo and Ake, were growing up. As the months went by, the Hammarskjolds discussed such things as the United States' entry into World War I, President Wilson's "Fourteen Points for Peace," the arrival of American troops in France, defeat after defeat for the Germans, and finally, in November 1918, the end of World War I.

Both Sten—now a student at Uppsala University—and Dag, still in preparatory school, gave good accounts of themselves in these family forums.

The year 1920 was a significant one in the life of Dag Hammarskjold. In January, when he was fourteen and a half, the League of Nations was formed in Geneva, Switzerland. Its purpose, according to its covenant, was "to promote international cooperation and to achieve international peace and security." League members agreed "not to resort to war." Instead, disagreements between nations would be settled by arbitration.

Hjalmar Hammarskjold agreed fully with the principles of the League of Nations. He had always taught his sons that war was useless. If the world was to survive, negotiation must take the place of fighting. It is quite likely that Dag, with youthful idealism, hailed the formation of the League of Nations as the dawning of world peace.

In the spring of 1920 another significant event in Dag's life occurred: Dr. Albert Schweitzer came to Uppsala.

Dr. Schweitzer was a great humanitarian who had dedicated himself to the service of humanity. He had given up an amazingly successful career of teaching, preaching, writing, and music to study medicine. Then he and his wife had gone to French Equatorial Africa and had built a hospital in Lambarene, where they treated thousands of suffering Africans.

During World War I, the Schweitzers, who were German citizens, had been treated as prisoners of war by the French. They had been forced to close their hospital. Finally, ill and penniless, they had been returned to their home in Alsace. Now Dr. Schweitzer was trying to raise enough money to go back to Africa and resume his humanitarian work. At the invitation of Archbishop Soderblom, he came to Uppsala to give a series of lectures at the university.

Dag must have found Dr. Schweitzer fascinating. His great burly figure, clad in a dingy black suit, and his big, shaggy head made him stand out in a crowd. But it was Schweitzer's brilliant mind, his great heart, and his philosophy of "reverence for life" that impressed Dag Hammarskjold most deeply.

"I am life which wills to live in the midst of other life which wills to live," Dr. Schweitzer said in his lectures. He had pledged himself to preserve and to promote life, rather than destroying or injuring it.

These lectures lighted a spark in the mind of fifteen-year-old Dag Hammarskjold. Later that spark would fuse together the beliefs his parents had implanted in him. His father had trained him to believe that no career was more worthwhile than one of service to his country, and his mother had taught him that all men are equal as children of God. If these two beliefs were to be put into practice, they must result in Christianity in action. That was exactly what Dr. Schweitzer was doing—translating Christianity into action.

For a while Dag considered studying for the ministry. By the time he was seventeen and ready to take the university examinations, however, he had decided to follow his father into government service.

Although Dag did extremely well on his university exams, he received no credit or compliments from his stern father. Mr. Hammarskjold did not believe in praising his sons.

"Ake did better," was Mr. Hammarskjold's cold comment.

For several years Ake Hammarskjold had been a dedicated public official, like his father. At the age of twenty-nine, he had been appointed secretary-general of the International Court at the Hague, Holland.

Young Dag and his brothers in 1920. From left to right: Bo, Dag, Ake, and Sten Hammarskjold

Bo, the eldest Hammarskjold brother, was in Swedish government service. Dag was very proud of his brothers.

In the summer of 1922, Bo took Dag with him on a mountain-climbing expedition in Silesia, in eastern Europe. It was Dag's first trip into the high mountains.

Bo, short and dark like his mother, must have been pleasantly surprised to discover that his youngest brother could easily keep up the pace he set. In spite of Dag's lack of experience in mountaineering, he was never the first to tire. Besides, he was the best of companions, cheerful, willing to do his share of camp work, obedient to commands on the trail, and quick to learn the rules of safety.

Dag loved the mountains. The beauty, the peace of the high altitudes, the fresh, clean air, the solitude— all these were soothing to the spirit and refreshing to the mind. When the expedition ended, Dag returned to Uppsala, eager to resume his studies.

3. "Signposts"

While attending the University of Uppsala, the oldest university in Sweden, Dag continued to live at home, instead of in the town as other students did. Wearing his smart school uniform, with the black-visored white cap that identified an Uppsala University student, Dag walked down the hill from the castle each morning and back up again each evening. Living at home set Dag apart from the other students, and so did his status as son of the lord lieutenant of the province. These circumstances increased his natural loneliness and reserve.

Dag's university courses that first year included history of literature, theory of philosophy, political economy, and French. Like his father he had a natural aptitude for languages, and he soon took up the study of several others. Before he finished his undergraduate work, Dag could read and speak French, English, and German, and classical Greek and Latin.

Dag was an excellent student, and he enjoyed all of

his classes. Thanks to his amazing memory, he could complete an assignment in half the time it took most of his classmates, yet get a top grade on it. Classmates often sought Dag out, climbing the hill to the castle to ask his opinion on some question of philosophy, political theory, or a mathematical problem. Dag's extraordinary memory was famous. He was considered a clear thinker and an impartial judge of student disputes.

At Uppsala University all students were divided into "nations," depending on which province they came from. These nations resembled American fraternities, each one having its own house, each forming a center for social life.

As citizens of Uppland Province, Dag Hammarskjold and Jon Soderblom both belonged to "Uppland Nation," the oldest one at the university. Although Dag attended few social functions given by his nation, occasionally he took Yvonne Soderblom, Jon's youngest sister, to one of the dances. Sometimes the two young people went sleighing. Throughout Dag Hammarskjold's life, he and Yvonne remained good friends.

Early in his university career, Dag began an independent reading program in modern and classical literature. He particularly liked Joseph Conrad, Thomas Wolfe, Herman Hesse, Thomas Mann, Emily Dickinson, and Katherine Mansfield. Often Dag read books in their original language, instead of in Swedish translations.

In the spring of 1925, when he was nineteen, Dag received his B.A. degree. He had set a brilliant scholastic record, but his father expressed no pride in his achievement. Instead, he reminded Dag of his own graduation.

"I took *my* B.A. when I was only eighteen," he said dryly.

About this time Dag began to keep a journal. It was not a day-by-day diary, listing what he did, nor did it contain observations on people and events. Rather, as he explained much later, the entries were "signposts you began to set up after you had reached a point where you needed them, a fixed point that was on no account to be lost sight of."

The occasional jottings in Dag's journal came out of his attempts to understand himself and his spiritual beliefs. Questions which his deep-rooted shyness and reserve prevented him from discussing with anyone else—even Archbishop Soderblom—found their way into his diary. Often he used mountain-climbing terms to express them.

During that summer of 1925, possibly near his twentieth birthday, Dag wrote a poem in his secret journal. It expressed a longing to make his character perfect and his family truly significant.

THUS IT WAS

I am being driven forward
Into an unknown land.
The pass grows steeper,
The air colder and sharper.
A wind from my unknown goal
Stirs the strings
Of expectation.

Still the question:
Shall I ever get there?
There where life resounds,
A clear pure note
In the silence.

Now that his undergraduate work had been completed, Dag took up graduate study in economics. Although he still lived at home with his parents, he took an active part in student activities.

In 1927 the "Uppland Nation," the fraternity-type organization to which Dag belonged, celebrated the 300th anniversary of its founding. Dag was elected "first curator," or chairman, of the celebration, probably in recognition of his remarkable scholastic record and his leadership qualities.

Neither graduate study nor college activities kept Dag from the outdoor sports he loved. Frequently he left Uppsala on Friday afternoon for a trip into the wilderness. Sometimes he went alone, but often a college friend, Per Olaf Ekelof, accompanied him. On his back Dag carried a rucksack which contained blankets, a cooking pot, oatmeal, raisins, and a book of poetry. A camera was slung from his shoulder.

The young men spent Friday and Saturday nights in mountain huts or out in the open, returning to town after two strenuous days of hiking.

On these trips Dag and Per Olaf discussed all sorts of subjects—philosophy, science, politics, books, art, and poetry. They did fully as much talking as they did hiking. However, Dag did not reveal to Ekelof or to any other college friend his deep feeling about spiritual matters.

After one of these camping expeditions, Dag wrote in his journal:

> Life yields only to the conqueror. Never accept what can be gained by giving in. You will be living off stolen goods, and your muscles will atrophy.

On long vacations Dag liked best of all to go on camping trips in Lapland. This thinly settled territory stretches across the north of Norway, Sweden, Finland, and Russia. It is mostly mountains, steep valleys, lakes,

Dag makes a speech to his fellow students at Uppsala University. Their white caps are a part of the traditional Uppsala uniform.

and rivers. There are few towns, few roads, and fewer railroads. More than half of Lapland lies within the Arctic Circle. This wild country of the midnight sun held a growing fascination for Dag. He would love Lapland all his life.

In 1928, not yet twenty-three, Dag received his master's degree in economics. At once he decided that a degree in law would also be valuable for a public official, and he started to read for it. He also joined a French club at the university in order to improve his French. Soon after he translated a play for the club to produce.

When the time came to cast the play, Dag was given a voice in the choice of players. For the leading feminine role, he chose Yvonne Soderblom. His fellow students were not in the least surprised. Everyone in Uppsala knew that Yvonne was the only girl who had ever interested Dag Hammarskjold. Besides, Yvonne was very attractive and talented, an excellent choice for the part.

In 1930 Dag's father, now sixty-eight, resigned his post as the lord lieutenant of Uppland Province and prepared to move to Stockholm. Dag, the only Hammarskjold son still at home, decided to accompany his parents. He had just received his law degree. Although the length of time normally required to obtain a degree in law was four or five years, Dag had earned his in only a year and a half. Now he wanted a doctorate in economics, but he could get that in Stockholm. Anyway, the capital city was the place for a future government servant to live.

As he prepared for a life in Stockholm, Dag wrote:

> What you have to attempt—to be yourself. What you have to pray for—to become a mirror in which, according to the degree of purity of heart you have attained, the greatness of life will be reflected.

4. The Road Begins

In the capital city of Stockholm, the Hammarskjolds rented an apartment facing a large park that surrounded the Royal Library. Immediately Dag began to study at Stockholm University for his doctorate in economics.

His father withdrew from active participation in government and devoted himself to the affairs of the Swedish Academy, of which he had long been a member. He spent most of his time in his study, reading books that had been recommended for the Nobel Prize in Literature. Occasionally he attended meetings of the academy.

Mr. Hammarskjold felt great personal satisfaction when his old friend and Uppsala neighbor, Archbishop Nathan Soderblom, was awarded the 1930 Nobel Peace Prize in recognition of his efforts toward Protestant cooperation.

Dag, too, was pleased. That same year he himself was offered a government job.

In the 1930s an economic crisis shook Europe. Low wages and unemployment caused much suffering in Sweden, and a Royal Commission on Unemployment was set up to find ways of easing the hard times. Dag Hammarskjold was asked to be secretary of this commission. He accepted, and thereafter his university studies took second place to his government work.

One of Dag's duties as secretary of the Royal Commission was to compile a report on unemployment. He persuaded the commission to encourage leading economists to write essays on different aspects of the unemployment situation. These papers would be added to the report as an appendix. Dag himself planned to write on economic ups and downs, as well as composing the main body of the report.

Dag made it a practice to write exactly four pages of the report each day. Some of his colleagues laughed at his industry, for he would return to his office late at night if he had been unable to complete his writing stint during the day. But Dag only smiled. The report would be long and technical, and he knew it would require many months of concentrated effort and steady writing.

Dag's work on the Royal Commission on Unemployment attracted much attention in Stockholm's financial circles. One of the men most interested in his work was Ernst Wigforss, minister of finance in Sweden's new Social Democratic government. Wigforss decided that Dag Hammarskjold was a young man worth watching.

The economics professors at Stockholm University

were keeping their eyes on Dag too. When the Bank of Sweden needed a secretary, its president asked a professor of economics at the university to suggest a young man suitable for the post.

"Dag Hammarskjold is your man," the professor replied.

Since Dag had almost completed his report for the Royal Commission on Unemployment, he accepted the position. From then on, he worked for the Bank of Sweden in one capacity or another until 1948.

Soon after Dag went to work for the bank, Minister of Finance Wigforss asked him to serve as principal clerk in Sweden's Finance Ministry. That was the beginning of Dag's double—sometimes triple—occupations.

The Royal Commission report, of 266 pages, was printed as a government paper in 1933. The title used was "The Spread of Boom and Depression." Dag submitted it to Stockholm University as his doctoral thesis in economics.

Wigforss complimented Dag on "The Spread of Boom and Depression."

"Is it your ambition," he asked his principal clerk, "to become a professor of economics and write further books on economic theory?"

Dag had no such ambition. "If I should take up writing seriously," he replied, "it would be along the line of practical economics, not theoretical."

Wigforss liked Dag's quick answer. When the undersecretary of the Finance Ministry resigned in 1936, Wigforss offered the job to Dag.

The position appealed to Dag. Undersecretary of finance was a civil service post, not an elective one, and it did not require affiliation with a political party. He had no wish to hold an office that involved running for election.

When Dag's name was proposed in Parliament for undersecretary of finance, objections were raised. That was the top civil service post in the Finance Ministry, and many members of Parliament felt that Dag Hammarskjold at thirty was far too young for such a responsible job. A proposal was made to divide the position and employ two undersecretaries, who would share the responsibility and the work. When Wigforss reported Parliament's sentiments to Dag, he agreed to think it over.

Dag consulted his father. Old Mr. Hammarskjold wasted no time in argument. He gave his advice in three words: "All or nothing."

His father's opinion confirmed Dag's own judgment. The next day he told Wigforss that he would not consider a divided position, and he was given the post of undersecretary with sole responsibility.

Wigforss and his new undersecretary worked together in perfect harmony. As the representative of the liberal party in power, Secretary Wigforss had the burden of defending his policies in Parliament and before the public. Dag, while still carrying on his Bank of Sweden duties, helped Wigforss formulate and carry out these policies.

In a remarkably short time, Dag made himself essential to Wigforss. Dag had a tremendous capacity for work, a brilliant mind, and a singular talent for winning people's cooperation. When there were differences of opinion within the department, Dag Hammarskjold was usually called on to mediate the arguments. He had a way of getting people to compromise and to emerge from the negotiations as friends.

Dag came to the city of Stockholm (below) as a student and remained to become a brilliant administrator.

Dag continued to live at home. He often saw his brothers Bo and Sten, who were living nearby. Bo held a government position in the Ministry of Social Welfare. Sten, who had gone into government service for a while, had retired from public life to become a writer. Ake had been abroad for about ten years, working for the League of Nations, and was only occasionally in Stockholm.

The League had not become a strong force for peace, as the Hammarskjolds had hoped. Lacking the means of carrying out its recommendations, the League of Nations became little more than an international debating society. Still, men like Ake Hammarskjold, who saw no better instrument for peace on the world horizon, continued to give it their best efforts.

In 1937 Ake fell victim to rheumatic fever. Soon he was dead, his brilliant career cut short at the age of forty-four. Ake's death was a terrible shock to his entire family. His father had apparently considered him the most brilliant of his sons and had expected great things of him.

Old Mr. Hammarskjold took pride in the fact that two of his sons were carrying on the Hammarskjold tradition of government service. However, as a life-long conservative, he could not have enjoyed the knowledge that his boys were working for an extremely liberal regime. Together the Hammarskjold brothers—Bo in the

Social Welfare Ministry and Dag in the Finance Ministry—were responsible for much of the legislation that transformed Sweden into a social welfare state during the 1930s. These laws made the government responsible for the health, education, and well-being of all the people.

Although Mr. Hammarskjold disapproved of the policies of the Social Democratic party, he understood that his sons were not necessarily radical in their personal views just because they worked for a liberal government. As he had always told his sons, a good public servant must put all of his ability and energy at the disposal of his country, regardless of which political party was in power.

Mrs. Hammarskjold was proud of Dag's success, but she feared he was being worked to death, since he spent such long hours at his desk.

Dag's office was a fifteen-minute walk from the Hammarskjold apartment. Every day he walked home for lunch and for dinner. If he was late leaving the office, he took a taxi home, rather than keep his mother waiting for ten minutes. Almost daily he stopped along the way home and bought flowers for her.

After the evening meal, Dag stayed with his parents for an hour or so, but by nine o'clock he returned to his office. Often he worked long past midnight, sometimes until the early hours of the morning.

Whenever Mrs. Hammarskjold met any of Dag's colleagues from the Finance Ministry, she begged them not to work her son so hard. The men always smiled at this request, because everybody in the department knew that Dag drove himself. He, and he alone, was responsible for the long hours he kept.

When a light was seen in the Finance Ministry at night, it was sure to come from Dag Hammarskjold's office. Whenever any official returned to the building to work in the evening and asked the night watchman if anyone else was around, the reply was sure to be, "Well, Mr. Hammarskjold is here, of course."

And yet, in spite of his long working hours, Dag managed to keep up with his hobbies. Somehow he found time for reading and for music. In winter he skied, and in summer he swam. He spent many weekends in the mountains of Sweden or Lapland.

Dag and a group of young men from the Finance Ministry took frequent weekend bicycle trips, riding from thirty to forty miles out into the country. When they reached the outskirts of Stockholm on the return trip, Dag always stopped and pulled on a pair of trousers over his shorts.

"It wouldn't do," he told his companions with a smile, "for some dignified member of Parliament to see the undersecretary of finance going around town bare-kneed!"

Dag's love of the outdoors and camping often took him into the wild and lonely northern lands. He is seen here in the Sarek Mountains of Sweden.

5. "The Scourge of War"

In the summer of 1939, Dag and Erik Swartling, an assistant in the Finance Ministry, took a long bicycle trip north into Norway.

Usually, when Dag escaped from the city, he left behind the problems of his office and worries over the international situation. Ordinarily he gave himself up to enjoyment of the crisp fresh air, the peace, the solitude, and the beauties of nature. That was why he found in hiking, bicycling, and skiing physical recreation and relief from nervous tension.

This trip was different. Dag could not dismiss from his mind the European political situation. Instead of pointing out to his companion the increasing sparseness of trees as they pedaled northward and identifying each plant and shrub they saw, Dag seemed not to notice the stark beauty of the north country. Erik, too, seemed lost in thought.

For six years Adolph Hitler and his Nazi party had been on the rise in Germany. Hitler's avowed intention was to "liberate" all Germans—the "master race" he called them—in whatever country they might reside. To this end he had already invaded Austria and Czechoslovakia.

A few months before Dag's bicycle trip, Germany and Fascist Italy had formed a political and military alliance. The previous week Germany had signed a nonaggression pact with Russia, a former enemy.

As Dag's strong legs propelled his bicycle northward, he must have considered what this unexpected alliance between Germany and Russia meant. There was only one logical conclusion: Hitler wanted to neutralize Russia so that he would be free to attack any of her neighbors he wished to "liberate."

Thoughtful government officials like Dag had no doubt that war was coming, probably a worldwide conflict whose scope would make World War I seem like a neighborhood quarrel. The only question was: When would the war begin?

One night Dag and his friend rested in the village of Elvirum, Norway. When they finished their supper, Dag did not take his book out of his knapsack, as he usually did on camping trips. Instead, the two men began to discuss possible escape routes for the Swedish king and key government officials, in case Hitler should invade Sweden.

The following day, in place of resuming the hike they had planned, Dag and Swartling spent their time searching for an escape route through the mountains to the North Sea.

They had just returned to Stockholm when the news

Dag had been fearing was splashed across the newspapers in great headlines. Hitler had invaded Poland on September 1, 1939. War had come!

Within a few days England, France, Australia, New Zealand, the Union of South Africa, and Canada had declared war on Germany. Russia invaded Poland, and that unhappy nation was partitioned between Germany and the Soviet Union.

Quickly the Scandinavian countries announced their neutrality, but Dag had no illusions about the value of such declarations. Hitler would not allow a proclamation of neutrality to stand in his way if he wished to invade a country.

In the spring of 1940, Dag's judgment was proved correct. In rapid succession the Germans invaded Denmark, Norway, the Netherlands, Belgium, and Luxembourg (all neutral nations), and then France. The Soviet Union invaded Lithuania, Latvia, and Estonia. Most Swedes assumed that Sweden would be next on the invasion list.

Of all the countries that had been overrun by invading armies, Norway drew the most sympathy from the Swedes. Although Sweden was officially neutral, most of her citizens were far from neutral in feeling. Many Swedes, including Dag Hammarskjold, did everything possible, short of endangering Sweden's neutral status, to help Norway's government-in-exile in London.

King Haakon of Norway and several important members of his government had escaped to England by way of the very route that Dag and Swartling had found.

Although neither German nor Russian armies entered Sweden, the country was practically isolated, surrounded by Nazi-occupied territory. As in World War I, shipping became difficult and dangerous, and supplies grew scarce. Inflation threatened Sweden, and Dag Hammarskjold was given the task of devising laws to establish price controls.

One day Dag was asked to fly secretly to London to discuss important economic problems with the Norwegian government-in-exile there. In a military plane, with several Norwegian diplomats, Dag began the dangerous flight over Norway and the North Sea. When the plane became airborne, Dag started to read.

Suddenly the pilot ordered, "Fasten your seat belts! A German plane has spotted us. I'm going to try to shake him."

The plane went into violent acrobatics, zigzagging, diving, climbing. Everyone in the airplane sat frozen, tense and terrified—everyone except Dag Hammarskjold, who continued to read calmly.

The crazy gyrations of the airplane ceased at last, and it resumed its normal flight pattern. The German plane had turned back as soon as the English coast had been sighted.

The other diplomats relaxed, greatly relieved at their narrow escape. Dag turned a page and went on reading. He had scarcely looked up from his book during the hair-raising experience they had just been through!

Dag's mission to the Norwegian government-in-exile was highly successful. Later on he was awarded the Grand Cross of the Order of St. Olav, the official Norwegian decoration, for his help during the war.

In 1940 Dag's mother died. As the youngest son and the only one at home during the latter half of her life, Dag had been very close to his mother. Her death left an empty space in his life that was never to be filled. She was buried in Uppsala, near the university.

For ten years Dag had written nothing in his journal. Now, in 1940, he resumed his occasional jottings, but neither the death of his mother nor the continuing horror of World War II was mentioned. Some of Dag's journal entries dealt with spiritual matters, and others concerned his constant quest for the "right road." He wanted his life to be one of service, and his present government work did not seem significant enough. He wrote:

The more faithfully you listen to the voice within you, the better you will hear what is sounding outside. And only he who listens can speak. Is this the starting point of the road toward the union of your two dreams—to be allowed in clarity of mind to mirror life and in purity of heart to mold it?

Dag continued to live with his aging father. Hjalmar Hammarskjold had been made chairman of the Nobel Foundation. This work absorbed all his energies, but he never lost his interest in government affairs and in the war. No doubt it pleased him that Sweden continued the tradition of neutrality that he had maintained with such difficulty during World War I.

World War II increased in fury, surpassing anything the world had ever dreamed of. Bombers, tanks, submarines, battleships, aircraft carriers, and mines caused widespread death and devastation. Millions of civilians and prisoners of war were killed in concentration camps. All over the world people recoiled in horror from the reports that filtered out of war-torn countries. To Dag Hammarskjold, who had come to accept Dr. Schweitzer's "reverence for life" philosophy, the wanton killing seemed unspeakably dreadful.

In May 1945 Germany surrendered, and the war in Europe was over. Three months later, following the dropping of atomic bombs on two Japanese cities, Japan surrendered.

Meanwhile a historic event had taken place. In the

Dag was deeply interested in the formation of the United Nations. Above, the United States representative signs the Charter of the new world organization.

spring of 1945, representatives of fifty nations had met in San Francisco and formed an organization which they named "The United Nations."

Dag followed radio and newspaper reports of the United Nations closely. The Charter, signed on June 26, created six principal bodies: a General Assembly, a Security Council, an International Court of Justice, an Economic and Social Council, a Trusteeship Council to control territories not yet self-governing, and a Secretariat to administer the United Nations.

The preamble of the Charter struck a high note, a note of faith and hope:

We the peoples of the United Nations determined

TO SAVE succeeding generations from the scourge of war, which twice in our lifetime has brought untold sorrow to mankind, and

TO REAFFIRM faith in fundamental human rights, in the dignity and worth of the human person, in the equal rights of men and women and of nations large and small, and

TO ESTABLISH conditions under which justice and respect for the obligations arising from treaties and other sources of international law can be maintained, and

TO PROMOTE social progress and better standards of life in larger freedom,

And for these ends

TO PRACTICE tolerance and live together in peace with one another as good neighbors, and

TO UNITE our strength to maintain international peace and security, and

TO ENSURE, by the acceptance of principles and the institution of methods, that armed force shall not be used, save in the common interest, and

TO EMPLOY international machinery for the promotion of the economic and social advancement of all peoples,

Have resolved to combine our efforts to accomplish these aims . . .

Dag read the entire Charter thoughtfully and hoped fervently that the United Nations would prove to be an effective force for peace. He would watch the progress of this new world organization with unflagging interest.

6. Swedish Diplomat

About the time World War II ended, Dag took an apartment of his own. It was a seven-room flat on the top floor of an ivy-covered brick building within walking distance of his father's home.

For the first time in his life, at the age of forty, Dag was living alone. Now at last he could indulge his tastes for modern art and classical music without having to consider someone else's comfort and wishes. He began to collect choice abstract paintings and records of his favorite composers—Bach, Vivaldi, Mozart, Mahler, Stravinsky, and Beethoven. He found Beethoven's *Ninth Symphony*, with its magnificent "Hymn to Joy," particularly inspiring.

Dag stopped in to see his father every day. Although the old man was eighty-three, his intellect remained as keen as ever.

After ten years as undersecretary of finance, Dag left this department of the Swedish government and went to the Foreign Ministry as a special adviser. Within a few years he was appointed secretary-general of the Foreign Ministry.

Great economic suffering, all over Europe, followed

in the wake of World War II, in spite of large loans from the United States of America. Dag was kept busy with all sorts of international economic negotiations, including trade agreements with the United States.

In 1947 the United States proposed the Marshall Plan as a method of helping war-torn countries. Each nation that wished to participate in the plan was required to submit a list of projects for which it wanted money. An Organization for European Economic Cooperation, known as OEEC, was to be set up to examine these projects, to eliminate duplication, and to ensure that the participating nations would help themselves and one another.

The OEEC meetings, held in Paris, began in 1947. Since Dag was now known all over Sweden as a distinguished economist and government servant, it was natural that he should be chosen to head the Swedish delegation. It was natural, too, that he should be elected vice-chairman of the OEEC executive committee. He played a leading role in the formation of the organization's charter, and in all negotiations that followed.

Since Sweden had not been invaded or bombed, she did not qualify as a participating nation in the Marshall Plan. Her role, as a traditionally neutral country, was that of a mediator, or peacemaker, and Dag Hammarskjold was an ideal delegate for that purpose.

It quickly became apparent that the requests for aid from the various countries of Europe added up to much more money than was available under the Marshall Plan. Dag was named to a group which was given the difficult task of getting the requests pared down to size.

One meeting after another was held with the representatives of the applicant nations. Lief Belfrage, Dag's colleague on the Swedish delegation, and Arne Skaug, head of the Norwegian group, were impressed with Dag's handling of these meetings. He seemed to have a clear and sympathetic picture of each nation's problems, and a realistic view of what could be done about

Dag Hammarskjold (middle) seated at the conference table of the OEEC in Paris

them. In every argument he took a neutral stand and held to it calmly and cheerfully, refusing to be swayed by angry protests or accusations.

One day a meeting was under way with the French delegation, whose members argued that France should have special concessions because of her tremendous losses in two great wars. Dag listened attentively.

Finally he broke in, speaking in flawless French. "What you are saying, gentlemen, is not reasonable."

Lief Belfrage and Arne Skaug exchanged amused glances. How often during these OEEC discussions had they heard Dag repeat that same charge, in the same quiet tone, with the same courteous smile.

Dag proceeded to point out the weaknesses of the French arguments and the rights of competing nations. With the unfailing cheerfulness he brought to every discussion, he suggested a compromise that would be just to all concerned.

The French representatives listened to Dag's persuasive words, but they were not willing to abandon their position. The meeting dragged on and on.

Finally Dag looked at his watch. He suggested that they all have dinner together, and then attend a play at a Paris theater. After the theater they could resume their discussions, fresh and rested.

"*You* may find a highbrow play restful," one of the delegates said. "But for me several hours of sitting in a theater listening to philosophical speeches does nothing whatever to clear my mind."

Others agreed, but Dag only laughed. His enthusiasm for the plans he had proposed for the evening carried them all along with him. The group trooped over to a small restaurant for a good dinner. As they ate, Dag took the lead in a spirited conversation about French culture. Then the group went to the theater to see the "highbrow" play.

Before the light of dawn filtered through the windows of the conference room, the French delegation had agreed to a compromise. Weary, but cheerful and friendly, the delegates separated to get a few hours of sleep before the next scheduled meeting.

The OEEC meetings continued for more than two years. Occasionally, during a recess, Dag and some of his friends would travel through France. Sometimes his companions were old friends from Scandinavia, sometimes new friends made during OEEC meetings. In either case, Dag acted as leader on the trips. Without benefit of guidebook, he instructed his companions in French history, literature, and culture. Was there any subject, some of them wondered, on which Dag Hammarskjold was not an authority?

Nearly every weekend Dag flew home to Stockholm to see his father and report to his superiors in the Foreign Ministry.

Old Mr. Hammarskjold found Dag's reports of the Marshall Plan negotiations very interesting. He pointed out that this was the first time in history that the nations of Europe had cooperated in anything except war.

During the course of the OEEC meetings, relations worsened between the Soviet bloc (Russia and her satellites) and the Western bloc (the nations of western Europe).

After the war, Germany had been divided into two parts: East Germany, occupied by the Soviets, and West Germany, occupied by the Allies. The capital city of Berlin had also been divided. Located in East Germany, it had been cut into East Berlin and West Berlin, half under Soviet domination and half under Western supervision. In June 1948, the Soviet Union halted traffic between Berlin and West Germany. Since the city was completely surrounded by Russian-controlled territory, no food or other supplies could be brought into West Berlin.

To meet this emergency, a gigantic airlift was organized by Western nations. At the rate of a plane every three minutes, vital supplies were flown into isolated West Berlin. This airlift, known as "Operation Vittles," continued for almost a year, when Russia finally lifted the blockade.

Incidents like the Berlin blockade convinced the Western world that trouble with the Soviet Union was inevitable. Several European nations signed a treaty pledging military aid from all of them if any one nation was attacked. The organization was named the North Atlantic Treaty Organization, commonly known as NATO. Sweden was urged to join, but she refused, on the grounds that such an alliance would endanger her traditional neutrality.

As the OEEC negotiations continued, many worthwhile projects were approved. The list included such things as draining swamps in Sardinia, building steel mills in France, constructing dikes in Holland, and laying out railroads in Turkey.

By the time the OEEC meetings drew to a close, and the Marshall Plan was in full operation, Dag Hammarskjold had earned universal respect from the delegates. He was admired for his intelligence, his good judgment, and his coolness in the face of attack. Most of all, delegates had been impressed by Dag's ability to find compromises which enabled opposing parties to "save face" and to remain on friendly terms. The negotiators for OEEC would not soon forget Dag Hammarskjold.

7. The "Right Road"

In 1951 Dag was made vice-minister of foreign affairs (equivalent to assistant secretary of state). He was now a member of the Swedish cabinet. As he had done in every post he had held, Dag often worked night and day. Of this obsession for work he wrote in his diary:

> Work as an anesthetic against loneliness,
> books as a substitute for people—!

In spite of many friends and numerous activities, Dag Hammarskjold was a very lonely man. He watched friend after friend fall in love and marry, while he himself remained solitary.

Dag was sometimes asked why he never married. He told a friend that he could never ask a woman to share his life. From observing his mother, he knew how hard it was on a woman to be married to a dedicated government servant, who was so often away from home.

In June 1952 Dag took a brief holiday, going alone on a camping trip into Lapland. As he always did before embarking on a journey, he told an assistant where he was going, so he could be located in case of an emergency.

With a light heart Dag hiked through the Lapland countryside that he had loved since his youth. The midnight sun made it possible for him to travel long hours. The wild beauty of the fjords, the valleys, the lakes, and the rivers was soothing to his soul. Equally restful was the solitude.

One afternoon as Dag swung along a faint track that led north, he heard the sound of an airplane overhead. It seemed out of place in this thinly settled land. No doubt the pilot was off his course.

Toward evening Dag reached the next village on his route. Like all other villages he had passed, this one was largely a collection of windowless huts, which were closed now while the owners were up in the mountains for the brief Lapland summer, tending their reindeer herds.

Besides the huts, the village had a handful of cottages, a church, and an inn. When Dag entered the inn, a man was waiting for him. It was the pilot of the plane he had seen, waiting to take him back to Stockholm.

Dag learned that the Russians had shot down two Swedish airplanes over the Baltic Sea. The Soviets claimed that the Swedish pilots were spies.

Sweden was up in arms over the incident. Dag's

presence in Stockholm was urgently needed. His superior, the foreign minister, was on vacation in Italy, and no one besides Dag had authority to act in this diplomatic crisis.

This was a serious situation, Dag realized. The righteous anger of his countrymen must not be allowed to trigger a war with the Soviet Union. The Soviets must be made to understand that such acts of violence could not be tolerated, yet they must not be pushed into a situation where war was the only way to save face. Dag hastened to board the plane for the flight back to Stockholm.

A few hours later, still in his hiking clothes, Dag entered his office in the Foreign Ministry. He had planned his strategy while on the plane, and he began at once to give orders. A note of protest was drafted and promptly sent off to the Soviet government in Moscow.

Dag and his staff waited anxiously for a reply. Hours dragged by. Other government offices closed. Still no answer came from the Soviet Union.

Finally, when the office should have been empty for the night, a telegraph message arrived. Dag smiled grimly as he read the Russian reply. He was sure the Soviets had deliberately delayed sending their answer, hoping it would arrive too late for the Swedes to act on it, but not too late to get their note in all the morning papers. That, of course, would give them an advantage in this diplomatic exchange.

Dag summoned his staff to an emergency meeting, and before dawn a counterreply had been sent to the Soviet Union. As long as the exchange of notes with the Russians continued, Dag saw to it that somebody was always on duty in the Foreign Ministry, so that the Soviet Union never had the advantage of the last word in the morning papers.

The members of NATO watched with mounting interest this battle of wits between Sweden and the Soviet Union. European diplomats hoped that Sweden would now join NATO and be a partner in the military alliance to protect European nations from Communist aggression. But Sweden did not. She had been neutral for more than 100 years, and neutral she remained.

Dag's masterly handling of the Soviet incident increased his fame. To the world he seemed the happiest of men, successful, respected, admired. Yet secretly, during that year of 1952, Dag was restless and uncertain. He had climbed as high as he could go in government service without allying himself with a political party, and this he did not want to do.

Where did he go from here, he wondered? None of the job opportunities suggested by friends appealed to him. Baffled in his search for the "right road," he became frustrated and unhappy.

A thoughtful moment on the balcony of the Foreign
Ministry in Stockholm

Over and over in his journal Dag brooded over his solitary condition:

What makes loneliness an anguish
Is not that I have no one to share my burden,
But this:
I have only my own burden to bear.

And again:

Pray that your loneliness may spur you
into finding something to live for,
great enough to die for.

Many of Dag's diary entries dealt with his overpowering need for a meaningful outlet for his many talents:

What I ask for is absurd: that life
shall have a meaning.
What I strive for is impossible: that my
life shall acquire a meaning.

No one knew of Dag Hammarskjold's journal. Many years later he told Lief Belfrage, his assistant in the Foreign Ministry, that he was keeping a diary.

"Someday I want you to take charge of it," Dag told his friend.

Before the end of 1952, Dag's mood of despair changed to one of hope and confidence. That summer he paid a visit to Yvonne Soderblom Anderberg and her husband in Gottland, and in December he went hiking with a Foreign Ministry colleague, Henrik Klackenberg, into the mountains. Something may have happened during one of these vacation trips to dispel Dag's mood of depression. On the other hand, the significant experience may have been a purely spiritual one. Since Dag told no one about it, and there is no hint in his journal of an important incident, it must remain a mystery. However, there is no doubt that *something* happened, for years later Dag wrote in his journal:

I don't know Who—or what—put the question, I don't know when it was put. I don't even remember answering. But at some moment I did answer Yes to Someone—or Something—and from that hour I was certain that existence is meaningful and that, therefore, my life, in self-surrender, had a goal.

From that moment I have known what it means "not to look back," and "to take no thought for the morrow."

Whatever caused the change in Dag Hammarskjold, by January of 1953 his journal entries reflected a hopeful, positive mood. His first 1953 entry was:

"—Night is drawing nigh—"
For all that has been—Thanks!
To all that shall be—Yes!

Dag Hammarskjold was ready to turn into the "right road" when it opened.

8. "The World's Most Impossible Job"

The "right road" opened for Dag Hammarskjold when he was nearly forty-eight years old. On April 7, 1953, the General Assembly confirmed his appointment as secretary-general of the United Nations. That night Dag wrote in his journal:

> To be free, to be able to stand up and leave *everything* behind—without looking back. To say *Yes*—

Two days later Dag emerged from a plane at New York's Idlewild International Airport. Without overcoat or hat, he stepped briskly down the steps, a slim, trim, youthful figure, with sandy hair and clear blue eyes. Two fellow countrymen, Ambassador Erik Boheman and Per Lind, a former Swedish Foreign Ministry assistant, followed him.

A crowd, composed largely of newsmen, waited to greet him. Cameras clicked and pencils raced.

Heavyset Trygve Lie, the retiring secretary-general, stepped forward to greet Dag. The two shook hands. Lie said, "Mr. Hammarskjold, you are taking on the world's most impossible job."

Retiring Secretary-General Trygve Lie greets Dag as he arrives in New York.

Dag smiled. Lie introduced him to the waiting newsmen, who then surged forward. He was asked to make
a statement for the press, and he complied. He said, in
part:

> I want to do a job, not to talk about it—
> not even afterward. . . .
>
> In my new official capacity the private
> man should disappear and the interna-
> tional public servant should take his
> place. . . .
>
> In articles recently published it has been
> said that I am interested in mountaineer-
> ing. That's true. . . . I have never climbed
> any famous peaks. . . . However, that
> much I know of this sport, that the qual-
> ities it requires are just those which I
> feel we all need today: perseverance and
> patience, a firm grip on realities, care-
> ful but imaginative planning, a clear
> awareness of the dangers but also of the
> fact that . . . the safest climber is he who
> never questions his ability to overcome
> all difficulties . . .

Asked about the pronunciation of his name, Dag
said, "You may call me *Hammershield,* if you like, since

that is what the name means. The correct pronunciation is *Hammarshuld.*" He did not know that soon the press—and the world—would simply call him "Dag."

With a courteous but purposeful expression, Dag began to push through the crowd. The rest of his group followed. It was clear to all newsmen that the first press conference of the new secretary-general was over. Obviously many reporters considered him a frustrating and puzzling subject.

Almost at once Dag learned that henceforth he would be accompanied wherever he went by a bodyguard. William Ranallo, who had been Trygve Lie's personal aide, had been detailed to guard Dag Hammarskjold. His orders were to be with the new secretary-general at all times, until relieved by his alternate.

Dag did not want a bodyguard. He was used to taking care of himself, and his privacy was very precious to him. However, he had no choice in the matter. Fortunately, he liked his aide at first sight. Ranallo was a big dark-haired police officer with a kind face, watchful eyes, and a strong body—a man to trust.

The following day Bill Ranallo drove Dag from his hotel to the UN Secretariat building, a towering glass structure on the bank of the East River in New York City. Dag was ushered into the great Assembly Hall, and up to the speaker's rostrum. Before the representatives of sixty nations and thousands of UN staff members, he took the oath of office:

I, Dag Hammarskjold, solemnly swear to exercise in all loyalty, discretion, and conscience the functions entrusted to me as secretary-general of the United Nations, to discharge these functions and regulate my conduct with the interest of the UN only in view and not to seek or accept instructions in regard to the performance of my duties from any government or other authority external to the Organization.

Dag then delivered his inaugural address in a quiet, almost conversational tone. In the course of his speech, he said:

I am here to serve you all. In so doing I shall count on your understanding, on your advice and on your will to give to what I have to say the attention that it may deserve. I am animated by a desire to meet all problems with an open mind. It is for you to judge how I succeed. It is for you to correct me if I fail.

Hammarskjold closed with a quotation from a Swedish poem: "The greatest prayer of man does not ask for victory, but for peace."

Dag expressed a wish to meet everybody who worked in the huge UN building, and to shake hands with each one. His executive assistant, Andrew Cordier, warned him that it would be quite a chore, since nearly 4,000 people worked in the Secretariat. The prospect of shaking 4,000 hands did not daunt Dag, however, and the tour was arranged.

For several hours on each succeeding day, John Cosgrove, chief security officer of the UN, conducted Dag from office to office, and from floor to floor. In each office the procedure was the same. Cosgrove introduced each staff member to the secretary-general, who shook hands and smiled. Occasionally Dag made a comment, but for the most part the ceremony was conducted in silence, except for the introductions.

The grueling tour ended five days later in front of the UN building.

"That's all, Mr. Secretary-General," said the chief security officer.

Dag turned to him and shook hands. "Thank you very much," he said.

Cosgrove looked Hammarskjold in the eye and abandoned protocol. "God help you, Mr. Secretary-General!" he said prayerfully.

The United Nations

Dag nodded. He knew that he faced a tremendous task and was going to need all the help he could get, both earthly and divine. He realized that a conscientious public servant is bound to make enemies. He wrote in his journal:

He who has surrendered himself to it knows
that the Way ends on the Cross—

For the first few months of his term as secretary-general, Dag's prime concern was his role as chief administrator of the huge UN Secretariat. As he phrased it, he intended to "put this house in order."

A few days after Hammarskjold's arrival in New York, FBI agents came to the Secretariat to continue their questioning and fingerprinting of Americans on the UN staff. This was part of the "loyalty investigations" by the United States government, to which Trygve Lie had objected.

Dag faced the agents with steely blue eyes. "You must leave at once," he said. "Do not return, for you will be refused entrance to any office in this house."

"But Mr. Secretary-General," the leader of the group protested, "we have permission to conduct these investigations. Mr. Trygve Lie . . ."

"The permission is withdrawn," Dag announced. "I am the secretary-general of the United Nations now.

No agency of any nation has or will have permission to invade these premises to question or investigate any member of my staff. When a person becomes an employee of the UN, he can be considered denationalized."

The FBI agent continued to protest. "Do you mean that accusations of subversive activities will go unchallenged?"

"I mean that such accusations must be brought to me," Dag replied. "We have a judicial process here. Each allegation will be examined and judged by strictly legal methods."

In spite of American protests concerning his stand, Dag remained firm. He refused to allow FBI agents inside the United Nations' offices.

Instead, Dag himself began to investigate thoroughly all UN staff members, to make certain that each one met his standards of "integrity, independence, and impartiality." As a result of his findings, some UN employees were fired and new people were hired to replace them. Gradually Dag built up, as he had in every position he had held since he first went into public service, a corps of competent, congenial, loyal assistants, whom he could trust. By the end of 1953, he had truly "put this house in order." The Secretariat was working smoothly in a well-ordered routine.

Among the personal aides on whom Dag relied

heavily were Per Lind, Ahmed Bokhari, Heinz Wieschhoff, Andrew Cordier, Ralph Bunche, and Hans Engen, Norway's permanent delegate.

Dag had worked with Per Lind in Sweden and knew his capabilities well. Heinz Wieschhoff, who had come to America from Germany in the 1930s, was an expert on African affairs. Bokhari of Pakistan served as adviser on the Far East. The American, Ralph Bunche, had intimate knowledge of both Africa and the Middle East, and he had demonstrated superb ability as a mediator in several UN crises. In 1950 he had been awarded the Nobel Peace Prize, the first black man to be so honored.

Andrew Cordier, another American, was Dag's executive assistant. He had been with the UN since its

The new secretary-general and his trusted adviser, Undersecretary Ralph Bunche of the United States

earliest days. He could be depended on for necessary background information, for protocol (or etiquette), and for objective assessments of world problems. Like Dag, Cordier combined unfailing cheerfulness, an excellent memory, and an enormous capacity for work. Together they made an effective team. Their mutual respect and affection deepened as time went on.

Dag was not prepared for the flood of publicity that was turned on his every official act. He often felt as if he were working in a goldfish bowl, and he did not like it. He preferred anonymity. He held frequent press conferences because they were expected of him, but he never enjoyed them. He didn't mean to be secretive about his work, unless secrecy was necessary for ultimate success. However, as he had told newsmen in the beginning, he "wanted to *do* a job, not talk about it."

On the subject of his private life, Dag flatly refused to speak. He held to his view that "the private man should disappear," and he maintained his right to have a private life out of the public eye.

It was not easy. Dag was accompanied everywhere by a bodyguard. Bill Ranallo drove him to the UN every morning, stayed on duty all day, and drove him home at night. Bill's wife Toddy spent many a lonely evening, because her husband often found it necessary to stay with the secretary-general until late in the evening, but she never complained.

Although Bill was Dag's faithful shadow, quiet and unobtrusive, he was far from colorless or neutral. Dag soon learned that Bill observed a great deal from his place in the background, and that his judgment of people and incidents could be trusted.

An apartment on East 73rd Street had been chosen for the new secretary-general before he arrived in New York. At once Dag set to work, refurnishing and redecorating it. He sent to Sweden for his books, his paintings, his favorite records, and a few treasured personal mementoes. Soon the eight-room, two-story flat was furnished in severely modern style, with streamlined Swedish furniture, except for an old-fashioned bird's-eye maple bureau that had belonged to Dag's mother. Above the fireplace hung a mountaineer's ice ax, given to Dag by a man who had climbed Mt. Everest. Art objects from Africa, Israel, and many other parts of the world added to the decor.

To manage the apartment, Dag had a housekeeper-cook called Nelly, and a butler, Ivar. However, Bill Ranallo acted as a sort of supervisor for the entire establishment, advising Nelly on menus and helping prepare dinner when Dag had guests.

Although Dag hated large parties and social chitchat, he loved to entertain friends in his apartment. His choice of friends reflected his varied interests. There were writers like John Steinbeck, Carl Sandburg, and

The secretary-general "at home" in New York

C. P. Snow, musicians like Pablo Casals, Fritz Kreisler, and Leonard Bernstein, and scientists like Robert Oppenheimer. These men and their wives, plus personal friends from the UN and from Sweden, were invited a few at a time for an evening of stimulating conversation and a gourmet dinner.

On the cook's night off, Bill Ranallo acted as chef, and Dag himself washed the dishes. His love of neatness was so strong that he could not be persuaded to leave the dishes for Nelly to do the next morning.

Far from resenting Bill's intrusion on his privacy, as Dag had feared in the beginning, he grew to enjoy the companionship of his loyal, practical bodyguard. Soon he looked on Bill Ranallo as a close personal friend, and an aide whom he could not do without.

9. The Best Birthday Gift

Although "putting this house in order" occupied most of Dag's attention during his first months at the UN, he kept well informed about trouble spots throughout the world. There were plenty of them. Each continent had its share.

An explosive situation had existed for a long time in the Middle East, where Arabs and Israelis were in constant conflict. Another tense situation had come up in Korea, which had been divided into two parts after World War II. In 1950 North Korean forces invaded and attacked South Korea. Sixteen UN member nations, including the United States, sent troops to South Korea to help repel the invasion. The People's Republic of China soon went to the aid of North Korea.

The Korean War lasted three years. An armistice agreement was signed on July 27, 1953, when Dag had been in office as secretary-general about three months. However, the agreement did not result in true peace. Numerous problems remained unresolved, some of which concerned prisoners of war. The United States was particularly unhappy about eleven American airmen whose plane had been shot down the previous January. The fliers were being held prisoner by Chinese forces, and the United States government charged that their imprisonment was a violation of the Korean Armistice Agreement.

Many other trouble spots around the globe claimed Dag's attention. There was no end to the study, the memos, and the conferences required for him to keep abreast of the problems of the world.

Each morning when Dag arrived at the Secretariat, he found great mounds of papers on the desk that had been clear when he left the night before at 8:00 or 8:30. Besides the important data on international questions, there were apt to be requests for the secretary-general to make speeches to various organizations. There were always numerous invitations, some to diplomatic functions, others to social affairs. Once he received thirty-five letters from a class of schoolchildren asking questions about the United Nations and its operation!

In spite of his busy schedule, Dag dealt promptly with every paper that was laid on his desk. He wrote a personal reply to the class of schoolchildren. Social invitations were refused and diplomatic ones accepted. International matters were taken up with his staff, and the necessary negotiations begun.

Dag gave each political problem not only keen intellectual analysis, but private prayerful consideration as well. In his journal he wrote:

Not I, but God in me.

And again:

If only I may grow: firmer, simpler—
quiet, warmer.

United Nations' prestige had declined in previous years. An article in a national newsmagazine proclaimed, "The UN is dying." Dag knew that many international problems were never brought to the attention of the United Nations. He wanted to change that situation and the world image of the UN, but he knew it would take time.

In October 1953, when Dag had been in New York for six months, his father died, at the age of ninety-one. Hjalmar Hammarskjold's death left a vacancy in the Swedish Academy, whose membership was always kept at eighteen. For the first time in the 200-year history of the academy, a son was elected to succeed his father.

According to custom, each new member of the Swedish Academy gives a speech honoring the life and accomplishments of his predecessor. Dag labored for days preparing his academy speech commemorating his father. It was the most difficult speech he had ever been called on to write.

Dag had loved, admired, and respected his father greatly, and he mourned his death sincerely. Yet he had resented him too. As he wrote to his artist friend, Bo Beskow, "I myself stand in the center in a perpetual conflict with a dominating father-image (in many ways deeply unlike me) whose pressure I hated and whose weaknesses I consequently saw very clearly."

Dag flew to Sweden to deliver his speech to the Swedish Academy and the assembled dignitaries of Sweden, including the king. In his address Dag pictured Hjalmar Hammarskjold as a moving force in Swedish government, and chronicled his father's half century of outstanding public service.

Although Dag characterized Hjalmar Hammarskjold as an authoritative man, with a reputation for extreme conservatism, much of what he said about his father applied equally to himself. For example:

> Hjalmar Hammarskjold was one of those who are firm in their roots and firm in their faith, those whose changing fates may well deepen the convictions and directions of their early years, but not change them. . . .

A mature man is his own judge. In the end, his only form of support is being faithful to his own convictions. The advice of others may be welcome and valuable, but it does not free him from responsibility. Therefore, he may become very lonely. Therefore, too, he must run, with open eyes, the risk of being accused of obdurate self-sufficiency . . .

The summer before his father's death, Dag had bought a farmhouse in Hagestad, on the southeastern coast of Sweden. The artist Bo Beskow owned a small cottage nearby.

The farmhouse Dag bought was 150 years old, built of whitewashed mud-brick, with a thatched roof. It had two rooms besides a kitchen. A barn and a hen-coop could be remodeled later for guest rooms.

Dag visited his Hagestad property in July 1954, when he returned to Sweden after a meeting in Geneva, Switzerland. Bill Ranallo was with him, and Dag and Bill took turns with the chores. However, Dag was apt to desert his floor sweeping and disappear outside to gather flowers for the table, to photograph a sunset, or to walk along the deserted beach and over the sand dunes.

Back in New York once more, Dag faced the usual

round of crises and decisions. Relations had become strained between the United States and the People's Republic of China because the Chinese still refused to release the eleven American airmen they had captured in January 1953. In November 1954 a Chinese Communist military regime tried the eleven fliers and sentenced them to long imprisonment as spies. All over America feeling ran high, and there were loud outcries for action against the People's Republic of China.

Dag's farmhouse near the sea in Hagestad, Sweden. The secretary-general spent as much time here as possible resting from the demands of his post.

On December 4, 1954, Henry Cabot Lodge, the United States' delegate to the UN, brought the matter of the American fliers to the attention of the General Assembly of the United Nations. A resolution, which condemned their trial and conviction as a violation of the Korean Armistice Agreement, was passed. The resolution authorized the secretary-general to make "continuing and unremitting efforts . . . by the means most appropriate in his judgment" to secure the release of the airmen.

As Dag walked through the corridor on the 38th floor of the UN building toward his office after the meeting, he must have been unhappy about the resolution. It pointed up a touchy situation that existed in the family of nations—the sore spot of the two Chinas.

Nationalist China had been one of the founding members of the United Nations and had held, from the beginning, one of the permanent seats in the Security Council. However, since the UN's formation, conditions in the Chinese nation had changed drastically. Communists had risen to power and had taken over mainland China. Nationalist China, the permanent member of the UN Security Council, now occupied only a tiny bit of territory, the island of Formosa. The Communist People's Republic of China claimed that it alone represented the Chinese people, that it should replace Nationalist China in the Security Council. So far, however, the People's Republic of China had not been admitted to membership in the United Nations.

Now the UN had commissioned Dag Hammarskjold to negotiate with the People's Republic of China for the release of the American fliers. But how could the Chinese Communist leaders be expected to honor any kind of a request from the United Nations when their government was denied a seat in the world organization? Besides, the resolution contained a paradox. It condemned the action of the People's Republic of China, yet it recommended negotiation. That combination was impossible, Dag believed. "You either condemn, or you negotiate. You can't do both," he said.

After careful study of the situation, Dag decided not to forward the UN resolution to Chou En-lai, premier of the People's Republic of China. Any action he took in regard to the American airmen would be on his own initiative as an individual.

Dag sent the Chinese premier a cable saying that he would like to talk to him in person about the American fliers. Chou cabled back, "In the interest of peace and relaxation of international tension, I am prepared to receive you in our capital, Peking, to discuss with you pertinent questions." Dag noted that Chou did not commit himself to a discussion of the airmen.

Dag prepared for the journey by briefing himself on the man with whom he would be negotiating, on the country he was going to visit, and on the entire political situation in the Orient.

On a bitterly cold day in January 1955, Dag arrived in Peking. Newsmen noted that for once he wore an overcoat and a hat. Among the staff that accompanied him were Dr. Bokhari, his Far East expert, and his faithful bodyguard, Bill Ranallo. The Chinese received Dag and his party with great courtesy.

The first meeting between Dag Hammarskjold and Chou En-lai was held in the splendid hall known as the Hall of the Western Flowers. Dag and Chou En-lai sat at the end of the hall, with the others seated on either side of them at long, low tea tables. For thirteen and a half hours, during four afternoons, the conversations continued.

Dr. Bokhari reported later that he was impressed by the earnestness of the atmosphere. Except for the attendants who moved quietly around the tables serving tea to everyone, there was no sound in the great hall other than the voices of the speakers.

Dag's first problem was to find a way of persuading the Chinese premier to discuss the matter of the American airmen. Chou considered it a purely domestic matter, not an international question, and he made it plain that he would allow no interference in Chinese internal affairs.

During the course of the four-day talks, Dag managed to convey to Chou that, while the conviction of the American fliers might be a domestic affair to China, it could have extremely serious effects abroad. He admitted that he had no right to meddle in any nation's internal affairs, but he pointed out that on the basis of the UN Charter, he was entitled to discuss any matter that might affect the international situation adversely. Chou accepted this position at last, and Dag proceeded to explain the American viewpoint on the airmen incident.

The talks were very involved and very, very subtle. In the oriental fashion, Chou used extremely indirect language. Dag, who had often been accused, especially by American reporters, of vague, theoretical speech, found this tendency valuable in his negotiations with the Chinese leader. They spent more time talking about Chinese art, Chinese philosophy, and Chinese history than they did about the fliers and other international political problems.

Dag's stay in Peking was not all business. He was entertained royally. Between talks there were dinners, receptions, and tourist excursions, on which Dag walked at his usual terrific pace.

One dinner given by Chou En-lai in Dag's honor consisted of ten courses, with many different dishes. Dag ate swallow-nest soup, shark's fin, and other oriental delicacies.

Dag and Chou En-lai of the People's Republic of China. They dined, chatted politely—and conducted delicate negotiations.

He wrote to Bo Beskow later, "The China voyage was a fantastic experience. . . . My working team was first class. Bill was great and he saved the morale both in my professors and the others when the wind blew so sharp that only the most open, simple human sense of humour and warmth could prevent frostbites." Undoubtedly the "wind" he referred to was the political climate.

Back in New York, Dag held a press conference, as he was expected to do. But he said nothing that he was expected to say.

"The door has been opened," was all he would reveal

about the negotiations with Chou En-lai, "and can be kept open, given restraint on both sides."

Reporters asked what he meant by that.

"No reacting prematurely," Dag explained. "No blasting away. One of the most curious and most upsetting features about the present world situation is that everybody is afraid of everybody."

Months passed and nothing happened in regard to the airmen. American feeling against the People's Republic of China mounted higher and higher. Dag quietly urged United States officials to continue to "keep the door open." He knew it was essential for the Chinese to "save face." If the fliers were to be released, it must not seem that the People's Republic of China had been pressured into this action.

In the spring of 1955, Dag began to make plans for the celebration of his fiftieth birthday. Anniversaries and birthdays were always very important to him, both his own and his friends. His fiftieth birthday, in particular, would be a very significant milestone.

A busy summer had been scheduled for Dag. The United Nations would commemorate its tenth birthday in June in San Francisco, and naturally the secretary-general was expected to attend. Dag had promised to deliver the commencement address at Johns Hopkins University, and to give lectures at Stanford University and the University of California. In August he must be in Geneva, Switzerland, to make a speech at an international conference on the peaceful uses of atomic energy, later known as the atoms-for-peace conference.

July, however, seemed relatively free from commitments, and Dag hoped to spend a couple of weeks at his country home in Sweden. He wrote about his plans to several Swedish friends, including Uno Willers, librarian of the Realm.

When Dag arrived in Stockholm in July, Willers reported a recent conversation with a member of the Chinese embassy. The oriental diplomat had inquired about the health of the secretary-general. Upon being informed that Dag intended to come to Sweden late in July to celebrate his fiftieth birthday, the Chinese gentleman observed that the news was "very interesting."

"What," he inquired, "would the secretary-general like for his birthday?"

"Books, Chinese paintings, or art objects," Willers replied. "But most of all, I think he would like the release of the American fliers."

The Chinese diplomat made no further comment, but twice someone from the Chinese embassy phoned to check on the date of Dag's birthday.

Dag and his faithful shadow, Bill Ranallo, arrived in Hagestad late at night on July 23, 1955. The artist, Bo Beskow, and his wife Greta welcomed them warmly.

The next few days were marvelously relaxing ones for the worn secretary-general, who had been involved in delicate diplomacy and official duties for so long.

Beskow, Greta, Dag, and Bill spent many happy hours together. Bill, who always carried a service revolver when he was on duty, taught Greta to shoot. He also worked happily for hours at a time on Dag's old car. All four swam and played games on the beach. Dag and Bo talked endlessly about art, books, music, nature study, photography—anything but international politics. Frequently Dag pulled the others to their feet and insisted on everybody taking a long brisk walk with him along the beach or over the sand dunes.

Bill Ranallo enjoyed everything about the vacation except the walks. He hated to walk fast, and he constantly tried to slow down the energetic secretary-general by pointing out things to be photographed.

"Look, sir," Bill would exclaim, as if delighted at an unexpected discovery. "What bird is that?"

Dag always knew the answer. He would pause long enough to name the bird and take its photograph. Then he would be off again, striding along as if he wore seven-league boots and must circle the world in a few hours.

Soon a red-faced, puffing Bill would exclaim, "That's a strange flower, sir. Have you taken a photograph of it?"

Again Dag would stop and focus his camera, and Bill had a chance to catch his breath.

On Dag's rare, brief visits to Sweden, he was always pestered by reporters and photographers. Even at his isolated beach house, this was a problem. Enterprising photographers tried to climb through the windows to get candid camera shots of the UN secretary-general.

As Dag's fiftieth birthday drew near, Beskow and Greta made plans to foil the newsmen who would certainly descend on the secretary-general that day.

At eight o'clock on the morning of July 29, after mugs of hot coffee and slices of the traditional Swedish birthday cake, Beskow and his wife took Dag and Bill down to the nearby harbor of Kaseberga. They boarded a small fishing boat that Beskow had chartered.

On board the boat the little group fished happily for cod all day long. Their lack of fishing success did not bother them in the least. At noon they ate a picnic lunch that Greta had packed, and then they returned to their fishing and their sunbathing.

When the peaceful day neared its end, the boat returned to port. But the little harbor of Kaseberga looked nothing like the deserted bay the "fishermen" had left behind that morning. Now the hills all around the village were covered with people. Men, women, and children cheered and sang as the Beskows' boat approached the wharf. Many were waving flags.

The instant the boat docked, Dag muttered glumly to Bill, "Let's get out of here." Dag and his bodyguard pushed through the crowd, with the Beskows following. The people cheered loudly as they passed.

A stack of mail awaited Dag at the cottage. There was a telegram in the pile, and he tore it open. It was from Chou En-lai.

"Happy birthday," the telegram said in part. "I am releasing the American airmen."

This was the best possible birthday gift! In his journal Dag wrote:

God sometimes allows us to take the credit—
for His work.

10. An Army to Prevent Fighting

In his speech at the University of California earlier that summer, Dag had said:

> It has rightly been said that the United Nations is what the Member nations make it. But it may likewise be said that, within the limits set by government action and government cooperation, much depends on what the Secretariat makes it.

In his handling of the American airmen incident, Dag had demonstrated the truth of this statement. He had strengthened the office of the secretary-general.

Member nations of the UN suddenly realized this. In Dag Hammarskjold, they saw, they had an effective instrument for personal arbitration, and they hastened to dump problems in his lap. Of this new willingness to "leave it to Dag," Hammarskjold wrote in his journal:

> Thanks to your "success," you now have something to lose. Because of this—as if suddenly aware of the risks—you ask whether you, or anyone, can "succeed."

Some of the most explosive world problems, that year of 1955, concerned the Middle East, especially the young State of Israel.

Eight years earlier, in 1947, the United Nations had partitioned Palestine into an Arab state, a Jewish state, and an international regime for the city of Jerusalem. For more than half a century, Jews from all over the world had been settling in Palestine, the homeland of their people in biblical times. This movement, known as Zionism, had accelerated greatly during and immediately after World War II. Following the partition of Palestine by the UN, the Jews formed their own state, called Israel. This action aroused bitter antagonism in the Arab world, because Arabs had claimed Palestine as their homeland for more than 1,000 years. They did not feel that any part of it should become a Jewish state. Immediately Israel was attacked by the four Arab states that surrounded her—Syria, Lebanon, Jordan, and Egypt—and by another Arab state, Iraq. The new nation was like a Jewish island in an Arab sea, but she fought desperately for survival.

Efforts by the United Nations to make peace between Jews and Arabs were not entirely successful. Armistice Agreements, negotiated by Ralph Bunche for the UN, were signed by Israel and four of the five Arab nations in 1949. However, the Arabs still refused to accept the presence of the State of Israel in the Middle East, so

A special agency of the UN was set up to care for Arab refugees in camps like Dekwaneh in Lebanon.

the agreements resulted only in an uneasy armed truce. This was frequently broken by Arab commando attacks on settlements just inside the border of Israel and by Israeli counterattacks.

Another problem was the presence of large numbers of Arab refugees in the Middle East. During the 1948 war, hundreds of thousands of Arabs had fled from Israel. Arab nations would not take them in, declaring that they belonged in Israel. The government of Israel was willing to compensate the refugees for their land, but it would not permit them to return, fearing that they would be a danger to the security of the new state. Miserable and homeless, the refugees were kept in United Nations' camps. The Arabs blamed the Israelis for the plight of these displaced persons; the Israelis blamed the Arabs; and both Arabs and Israelis blamed the United Nations for failing to find a quick, satisfactory solution for the refugee problem.

When Dag Hammarskjold became secretary-general of the United Nations, the quarrel over the refugees was as far from settlement as ever. By that time the number of Arab refugees approached the million mark.

There were other sources of trouble between Israelis and Arabs. The matter of shipping through the Suez Canal caused much bitterness. The canal was in Egyptian territory, but according to the Suez Canal Convention of 1888, it was an international waterway. Therefore, when the Arab nation of Egypt closed the canal to shipping destined for Israeli ports, Israel complained to the United Nations. The Security Council adopted a resolution calling on Egypt to end her restrictions against Israel, but the Egyptians did not comply. Again and again Israel protested to the United Nations, yet Arab ports and waterways continued to be closed to Israeli shipping.

When Dag had held his UN post for about a year and a half, a new leader, Gamal Abdel Nasser, arose in Egypt. He soon became a powerful spokesman for all Arabs, not just for Egyptians. Nasser vowed to destroy the State of Israel completely and return Palestine to the Arabs.

In January 1956 Dag made a long tour of the Middle East, Australia, and the Orient. He visited some fourteen countries, including Israel and Egypt, talking to the leaders and gaining firsthand knowledge of the people and their problems. In the Middle East, Dag saw for himself that the Arab-Israeli Armistice Agreements, which Ralph Bunche had negotiated in 1949, were being violated by both Arabs and Israelis.

Dag returned to New York convinced that the situation in the Middle East was critical. The members of the Security Council realized this was true. In a proposal put forth by the United States on March 20, 1956, the council requested the secretary-general to go to the Middle East and "reestablish compliance" with the 1949 Armistice Agreements.

Dag knew exactly what was expected of him. He was to pull both Arabs and Israelis back from the brink of war. It would be a difficult task, if not an impossible one. Nevertheless, Dag was willing—even anxious—to try. He flew to the Middle East, taking with him an adviser, George Ivan Smith, and his bodyguard, Bill Ranallo. They spent the month of April in the Middle East, shuttling back and forth from one country to another.

Dag talked with David Ben Gurion, prime minister

of Israel. Ben Gurion was a well-educated, dynamic person, and intensely patriotic. He explained that his people, the Jews, had held this land for many centuries until driven out during the days of the Roman Empire, nearly 2,000 years before. It was just, he maintained, for the Jews to have their own nation here. It was right for them to return to the land that God had given to their ancestor Abraham at the beginning of Jewish history.

Ben Gurion enjoyed discussing art, literature, and philosophy with the UN secretary-general. The two cultured statesmen talked for hours over "oceans of tea," alternating political matters with other topics.

Dag also had many conversations with Arab leaders, especially with Nasser and his foreign minister. Nasser was dedicated to the complete destruction of Israel. The Jews had no right in Palestine, he maintained, because the land had belonged to the Arabs for centuries.

At one of his meetings with Nasser, Dag thought an understanding had been reached on a vital point of the Armistice Agreements. Yet when he arrived at the Cairo airport, he learned that Nasser was circulating a contradictory report.

Dag directed Ranallo to take him right back to Nasser's office. He demanded—and got—an immediate audience with the Egyptian leader.

Usually calm, controlled, and courteous, Dag

Hammarskjold could be angry and outspoken when the occasion called for it. This was one of those occasions.

"You are completely mistaken," he told Nasser bluntly, "if you think I am to be satisfied with the appearance of an understanding."

Thus pressured, Nasser confirmed the original understanding. Dag promptly released a statement to the press, to prevent Nasser from changing his mind again.

Back in New York early in May, Dag reported to the Security Council on what he had accomplished. He had secured written agreements from Egypt, Israel, Jordan, Syria, and Lebanon for an unconditional cease-fire. Border violence in the Middle East had been brought to an end for the present.

Security Council members praised Dag highly. The French ambassador said, "War has not broken out in Palestine. Mr. Hammarskjold's stature has been increased by the test to which we subjected him, and the same applies to the prestige—which I know to be dearer to him than his own prestige—of his office."

But Dag did not waste time in self-congratulation. He wrote in his journal:

> What next? Why ask? Next will come a demand about which you already know all you need to know: that its sole measure is your own strength.

To a reporter who accurately judged the Arab-Israeli cease-fire to be only a partial solution of the Middle East problem, Dag replied:

> There are quite a few situations where we must live and learn to live with provisional arrangements, because there is no solution to the long-range problems which we can find overnight. We must simply grow into the solution . . .

Dag was anxious now to get on with the other problems of the Middle East. Chief of these were resettlement of the Arab refugees, agreement on water rights to the Jordan River, which flowed through Arab-Israeli boundaries, and disarmament of the demilitarized zones. In July he returned to the Middle East for negotiations.

For months Dag had been driving himself to the limit of his strength. His "quiet diplomacy" went on almost day and night, allowing him little rest. He had planned to go to Sweden that summer for a few days of peace, and he had already written to his friend Beskow:

> . . . Bill and I hope to come around the 25 of July for a few days, but . . . everything depends on Ben Gurion's maneuvers (alas!) . . .

However, it was not Ben Gurion, after all, who spoiled Dag's plans for a birthday vacation in Sweden. Late in July, while Dag and Bill were in Israel, they heard shocking news: Nasser had nationalized the Suez Canal!

Dag wired Beskow: "Visit to Sweden canceled. . . . Reasons obvious . . ." He flew back to New York for an emergency meeting of the Security Council.

The Suez Canal forms a waterway 103 miles long across Egypt, connecting the Mediterranean with the Red Sea. Use of the canal reduces a journey from Europe or America to the Persian Gulf by 5,000 miles or more, and saves thousands of dollars. Thus the Suez Canal is very important to the world's shipping.

Soon after its opening in 1869, the Suez Canal came under the financial and administrative control of Great Britain and France. In 1888 the Suez Canal Convention was signed by the representatives of nine nations, including the ruler of Egypt. The convention stated that the canal "shall always be free and open, in time of war as in peace, to all ships of commerce or of war, without distinction of flag." Thus, Nasser's move in nationalizing the canal and closing it to shipping except on his own terms was held by many nations to be a violation of international agreement.

A number of things may have influenced Nasser to take this drastic step. Undoubtedly he felt that Egypt did not get her fair share of the Suez Canal's profits. In addition, he resented the fact that the United States and Great Britain had both withdrawn their offers of aid in building the proposed Aswan High Dam on the Nile River. Whatever his reasons, on July 26, 1956, Nasser announced, "This canal is ours. We shall use that money [revenue from tolls] for building the High Dam. We shall rely on our strength, our own muscle, our own funds."

At once England and France filed official protests against Nasser's action. After futile attempts at arbitration, the matter was taken to the Security Council of the United Nations. Under Dag's diplomatic leadership, six general principles were finally decided on, but a resolution to carry them out was vetoed by the Soviet Union.

As the weeks passed, tension mounted. Great Britain froze Egyptian assets in the United Kingdom, and the United States did the same in America. Egypt sank ships and barges in the harbors at both ends of the Suez Canal and in the canal itself. Months would be required to clear the waterway for ship traffic.

On October 29 Israeli troops, in a swift assault, invaded the Sinai Peninsula, and fighting between Israel and Egypt followed. The governments of Great Britain and France issued an ultimatum to Egypt and Israel, warning them to stop fighting, to withdraw at least ten

These British troops fought their way into the Egyptian city of Port Said to gain control of the Suez Canal (below). Notice the hulls and masts of sunken ships.

miles from the canal within twelve hours, and permit British and French forces to occupy the canal zone.

The ultimatum was ignored. British and French troops promptly landed in Egypt, and their planes attacked Egyptian airfields.

By November 2, Israel controlled nearly all of the Sinai Peninsula and had occupied Gaza. British and French troops now held about one-fourth of the canal's banks, and their governments announced that they would continue their "police action" until the fighting stopped.

During these weeks of attack and counterattack, of accusation and counteraccusation between nations, Dag Hammarskjold and the UN Security Council had made

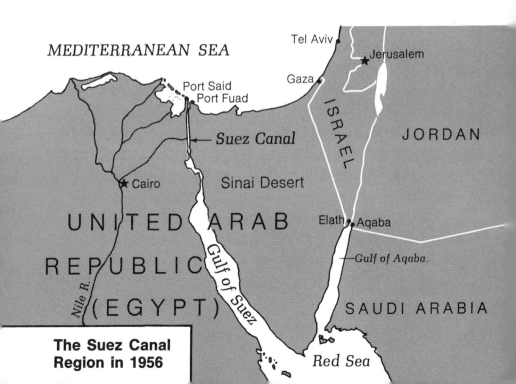

The Suez Canal Region in 1956

many attempts to find a peaceful settlement to the quarrels. Whenever a resolution was proposed in the council, however, one or another of the permanent members would veto it, and no action could be taken. Finally the matter was referred to the General Assembly, where action cannot be blocked by a single veto.

In the early morning hours of November 2, the General Assembly passed a cease-fire resolution, with six members abstaining from voting.

Lester Pearson of Canada explained to the assembly why he had refrained from voting on the measure. There was "one great omission" in the resolution, he said. He would have liked to see a provision authorizing the secretary-general to establish a UN army, which would be a "truly international peace and police force."

On Saturday, November 3, the General Assembly made good this omission. Dag Hammarskjold was authorized to submit within forty-eight hours a plan for a United Nations police force. Immediately Dag set to work on this extremely difficult assignment.

As if the Suez crisis were not giving the United Nations enough trouble, at the same time a rebellion broke out in Hungary, which was a satellite of the Soviet Union. Hungarian rebels demanded free elections, freedom of the press, the withdrawal of all Soviet armed forces, and abolition of the secret police. Instead of withdrawing, the Soviet Union promptly sent more troops into Hungary, encircling Budapest and sealing off the frontier with Austria. Tanks were brought in to crush the rebellion of the Hungarian freedom fighters.

A Soviet veto prevented any action in the UN Security Council on the Hungarian question, so the matter was taken to the General Assembly. The assembly called on the Soviet Union to withdraw its troops from Hungary. It requested Dag to investigate the situation, and it asked Hungary and the Soviet Union to permit UN observers to enter the strife-torn nation.

Between his assignment to set up the UN Emergency Force (UNEF) within forty-eight hours and his efforts to find a basis for negotiation between the Hungarian freedom fighters and the Communists, Dag worked around the clock for days. Meeting followed meeting, and conference followed conference. Other men grew faint from fatigue, but Dag Hammarskjold remained alert and efficient.

When each night meeting adjourned about dawn, Dag always summoned his staff to his office for an informal discussion of what had been accomplished, and what remained to be done during the day that was dawning. At seven in the morning he went home to his apartment.

"I'm going to let you sleep," Bill said one morning, worried about the long strain under which his boss had been working.

"No," Dag replied. "Please wake me as usual: 8:30."

When Dag telephoned his good friend, Lief Belfrage, in the Swedish Foreign Ministry to request Swedish troops for UNEF, Belfrage asked, "Aren't you very tired?"

"Oh, no," Dag replied. "I don't think I've slept more than two or three hours this week, but I'm doing fine."

During this period President Eisenhower said of Dag Hammarskjold, "He has not only shown his ability. The man has displayed a physical endurance that is highly remarkable, if not unique. Night after night he has made do with one or two hours of sleep, and worked both day and night, and, I might say, worked with intelligence and devotion."

By November 7 the plans for organizing UNEF had been completed, and troops were dispatched to Egypt. It was the world's first army under orders not to fight, but to *prevent* fighting. Britain, France, Israel, and Egypt then agreed to a cease-fire.

Lester Pearson expressed the general feeling: "We may have been saved from the very edge of catastrophe by the action of the UN."

Dag wrote in his journal:

Without our being aware of it, our fingers
are so guided that a pattern is created
when the thread gets caught in the web.

11. A Place to Be Quiet

One of the first things to be done when the Suez crisis had been safely passed was to clear the Suez Canal of the forty-eight ships, tugs, and barges that the Egyptians had sunk in it to prevent its use by other nations.

Dag gave the job of clearing the canal to a former chief of the United States Army Corps of Engineers, Lieutenant General Raymond "Jack" Wheeler.

Wheeler managed to clear the canal in four months, much faster than had been estimated. As a memento of his work, he wanted an autographed photo of the UN secretary-general. Although Dag's secretary told Wheeler that the secretary-general never signed his photographs, the general took a photo to Dag's office.

"Mr. Secretary-General," he said, handing Dag the picture, "I'm told you never autograph your photos, so I'm giving you a chance to say *no.*"

Dag looked from the picture to the general. After a long pause, he smiled and signed the photograph.

The Suez crisis was over, but the Hungarian trouble

remained. The Soviet Union had moved into Hungary with more tanks and soldiers and had put down the uprising by force. The free world watched, sympathizing with the Hungarians, but making no move to help.

The Hungarian freedom fighters blamed Dag and the United Nations for failing to support them in their rebellion. There had been twenty-four hours, they pointed out, during which the secretary-general might have gone to Budapest and changed the course of events.

Dag felt no guilt, only a deep regret that he had been unable to help. The news of the Hungarian revolt had come when he had just been given a mandate to organize the UNEF within forty-eight hours. He had immediately appointed an Investigating Committee to be sent to Hungary, but the Communist government of that nation had refused to admit the committee. At that particular time, it had been physically impossible for the secretary-general to do anything more.

As soon as the UNEF had been organized and dispatched to Egypt, Dag announced plans to go to Budapest himself. However, the Communist government would not allow him to enter Hungary, so he was helpless to act.

During the stormy UN sessions concerning Suez and Hungary, delegates from various countries had shouted furiously at one another, and Dag had sometimes felt that he could not possibly preserve his calm manner any longer.

At times like these, Dag would slip quietly out of the room. Usually he would rush up to one of the abstract paintings that he had borrowed from New York's Museum of Modern Art and hung on the walls of UN corridors. He would stand before a painting for several minutes, until his nerves had calmed and he had recovered his self-possession. Then he would return to his place in the meeting hall, showing to the world his usual impassive face and poised manner.

The long strain of the Suez crisis taught Dag that he needed a place in which to be quiet, to refresh his spirit. He realized that his need must be shared by many others in the UN building. They, like him, were guiding the destiny of many people. The Secretariat should have a Meditation Room.

Actually, it already had one, but the room was seldom used. It was a tiny, dismal, almost triangular cubbyhole squeezed out of the public lobby in the General Assembly Hall. Dag decided to revamp it and make it beautiful and soul-soothing.

"This house must have one room," Dag said, "one place which is dedicated to silence in the outward sense and stillness in the inner sense . . ."

When Dag finished carrying out his ideas, the little

Meditation Room achieved the exact effect he wanted. Dag described it like this:

> . . . in the center of the room there is this block of iron ore, glimmering like ice in a shaft of light from above. That is the only symbol in the Room—a meeting of the light of the sky and the earth. . . .
>
> The original idea was one which I think you will all recognize . . . it is the empty altar, empty not because there is no God, but empty because God is worshipped in so many forms. The stone in the center is the altar to the God of all . . .

The end wall of the room needed a mural. It must be an abstract painting, for—as Dag said—". . . in a room of this kind in a house of this character we could not use any of the symbols with which man has been used to link his religious feelings."

Dag knew exactly the right artist to paint the mural —Bo Beskow. On August 12 Beskow and his wife, Greta, arrived in New York. For almost three months they stayed with Dag in his apartment on East 73rd Street, while Beskow worked on the mural.

The Meditation Room was opened to the public on November 8, 1957. Dag himself wrote the text of a

The Meditation Room

leaflet to be handed to every visitor to the room. Today a plaque hangs in the Meditation Room, with an inscription also written by Dag Hammarskjold:

This is a room devoted to peace and those
who are giving their lives for peace.
It is a room of quiet where only thoughts
should speak.

The Meditation Room has had millions of visitors since it was opened. Dag himself found it a refuge from the strain of his official duties. He visited it several times a week, and he never made a journey without first spending time in the Meditation Room.

Dag had been reelected to a second five-year term as secretary-general on September 26. When he began his second term the following April, he said in a statement to the press:

Service of the United Nations . . . is
profoundly meaningful—whether it bears
immediate fruit or not. If it paves one
more inch of the road ahead, one is more
than rewarded. . . . This is true whatever
setbacks may follow: If a mountain wall
is once climbed, later failures do not
undo the fact that it *can* be climbed . . .

In his speech Dag described the limits of the secretary-general's authority as spelled out in the UN Charter.

Article 99 of the Charter specifies that "the Secretary-General may bring to the attention of the Security Council any matter which in his opinion may threaten the maintenance of international peace and security." With this article in mind, Dag went on to say:

. . . I believe that it is in keeping with the philosophy of the Charter that the secretary-general should be expected to act also without such guidance [direction from the Security Council], should this appear to him necessary . . .

Probably few of his audience realized it, but with these words Dag Hammarskjold was announcing his intention to expand the functions of his office. In the future he would depend more and more on "quiet diplomacy."

As he began his second term, Dag wrote:

The best and most wonderful thing that can happen to you in this life is that you should be silent and let God work and speak.

About the same time that the Meditation Room was being prepared, Dag provided for himself another "quiet place." He rented a house about two hours' drive north of the city, near Brewster, New York. On the property was a small lake, surrounded by overhanging trees. To this rural retreat Dag and Bill (or Don Thomas, Bill's alternate) occasionally took a guest or two. The men swam, sunned themselves on a raft, practiced archery, took leisurely canoe rides, and fished in the lake.

Dag loved to fish; that is, he enjoyed standing on the shore of the little lake, holding a fishing rod. He liked to watch the light shimmering on the surface of the water, or the feathery clouds drifting across the sky, or the leaves of the trees trembling in the soft breeze. Once, to everyone's surprise, Dag caught a fish. But he could not bring himself to take it off the hook, and had to call Bill to do it for him.

After a weekend at Brewster—two days of wonderful peace and relaxation—Dag found it difficult to return to the hectic pace and the strain of his United Nations work. On the way back to the city one Sunday night, in the customary weekend traffic jam, Dag said to his companions, "When I keep going day and night without stopping, I somehow manage. But after a weekend like this, it seems impossible to face what I have to face at the UN."

12. "Let Dag Do It"

During the next few years, one crisis after another was brought to the attention of the United Nations—troubles in Tunisia, Algeria, Indonesia, Kashmir, Lebanon, Jordan, Iraq, and Sudan, besides many others. More often than not, the problems were turned over to Dag, to be dealt with in his own fashion. Increasingly the UN Security Council, in facing any quarrel between member nations, tended to say, "Let Dag do it."

This suited Dag Hammarskjold. He had learned that with his "quiet diplomacy" he could obtain results that were often impossible through other UN channels. Dag coined a new phrase to describe this means of easing trouble spots: "UN Presence."

In the Suez crisis the UNEF—an army to prevent fighting—had been a UN Presence. In a border dispute between Cambodia and Thailand, UN Presence took the form of a personal representative of the secretary-general, who went to the scene to help straighten out the matter. Lebanon complained that the United Arab Republic (a recent merger of Egypt and Syria) was interfering in her international affairs, and Dag sent a UN Presence in the form of a 100-member Observation Group to keep watch on the Lebanese borders.

"This," said Dag, "is a very good example of what UN Presence can mean in a very hot situation without any resort even to military units."

Soon Jordan, too, complained of United Arab interference and asked for protection by the United Nations. However, Jordan was unwilling to admit either armed soldiers or a large band of civilians. So Dag sent a single man, a civilian, as a sort of UN ambassador, to observe and to report to him.

When Laos asked the United Nations for help, Dag himself supplied the initial UN Presence with a personal visit to Laos. He was followed by a technical assistance mission. Other forms of UN Presence were

The UN Emergency Force on guard in the Sinai Desert —a striking example of UN Presence

sometimes supplied by the Economic and Social Council and the UN Special Fund. In addition, OPEX (Operational and Executive Personnel) assisted new nations with experienced administrative, operational, and executive personnel.

Dag summed up his "Presence" philosophy in this way:

> We have learned that UN physical presence is a new and decisive element in the solution of conflicts . . . through reconciliation. It may take varying forms. The forms must be chosen after careful analysis of the situation.

Dag's employment of UN Presence usually pleased the small nations. Little countries, weak but proud, preferred accepting help from the United Nations—their own organization—to being obligated to any of the Western or Eastern powers.

The attitude of the great powers often differed from that of little states. Sometimes they were happy to be relieved of responsibility for weaker nations, and sometimes they resented the growing role of the UN. Most of the time the United States cooperated with Hammarskjold, only occasionally opposing him when his policies conflicted with American interests. Great

Britain had originally resisted Dag's role in the Suez crisis, but she became more and more willing to let the United Nations bear the burden of keeping peace in the Middle East.

France, too, had objected to UN interference in the Suez affair. Unlike Great Britain, however, her opposition to Dag Hammarskjold's growing influence increased as time went on, rather than decreasing. When Charles de Gaulle came to power in France in 1959, he vowed to restore his country's strength and prestige to that of a great world power. He viewed with suspicion and resentment every move that strengthened the authority of the UN secretary-general.

The Soviet Union also resisted any enlargement of UN powers. Like other nations, the Soviets were inclined to applaud Dag's policies when they coincided with their own and oppose contrary policies. But some Soviet leaders liked Dag personally even when they resented his growing authority.

At the beginning of March 1959, Dag set out on a long inspection tour of potential and present areas of trouble in Asia. He visited Burma, Thailand, Laos, Cambodia, Malaya, Nepal, and Afghanistan. The tour ended, by invitation, in Russia. There, Dag was entertained by Nikita Khrushchev, the Soviet leader, who proved to be a genial host.

At one time during Dag's stay in Russia, Khrushchev

pointed to his foreign minister, Gromyko. "You know if I had listened to that fellow," Khrushchev said, "you would not have been here now. He thinks you're a Western agent and should not be permitted in the Soviet Union."

Another Russian diplomat spoke up. "Everyone is an agent, even if he comes from Sweden."

Quickly Dag retorted, "True, I was launched in Sweden, but once in orbit I do not come close to any country."

Khrushchev took Dag rowing on the Black Sea. The Soviet leader manned the oars, and Dag pointed out the direction. When the visit ended, Khrushchev said to his guest, "When I come to see you, we will row again, but then you will have to row, and I will tell you where to go."

"Well, in that case," Dag replied, "we will each take one oar!"

Dag had hoped to spend a couple of weeks in his Swedish farmhouse that summer, but all he could squeeze in was two weekends, between UN trips.

In November Dag was invited back to Laos, a sure indication of the wholehearted acceptance there of his UN Presence.

In December he began a long tour through Africa, visiting African capitals and talking and listening to leaders of the new nations. He went to Senegal,

Liberia, Guinea, Ghana, Togo, Nigeria, Cameroons, Congo, Ruanda-Urundi, Tanganyika, Kenya, Uganda, Somaliland (now known as Somalia), Ethiopia, Sudan, Egypt, Libya, Tunisia, and Morocco. All over Africa the UN Presence was obviously welcome.

From the beginning of his service to the United Nations, Dag had been aware of the importance of the emerging nations in Africa and Asia. When he first took office as secretary-general in 1953, there were only four independent African states in the UN. Now the number had more than quadrupled. By the end of 1960, the United Nations would include twenty-six African states! Dag called 1960 "The Year of Africa." In a speech in Somalia, he said:

> By the end of this year I think that the group of African nations will be one of the strongest continental groups in the United Nations and in the family of nations . . .

Dag realized that this great bloc of new nations could be a stabilizing force in the UN. If these young countries could be kept free from obligation to either Communist or democratic nations, they might become powerful enough, as a group, to match the strength of the so-called Great Powers.

However, in order to grow strong, the new states needed trained leaders, and they must build strong institutions. During his trip around Africa, Dag saw that a great deal of money would be required by young nations to establish schools, hospitals, and industries, and to train leaders, doctors, and engineers. He began to make plans for raising the necessary funds and providing the required training.

In June 1960 Dag flew to Nepal, a small country in Asia, at the invitation of the king and queen. During this visit Dag was permitted the great thrill of flying over the Himalayas, the highest mountains in the world. He took many photographs. From his youth Dag had been an avid and skilled photographer, and he considered these pictures to be among his best.

While Dag was in Geneva, Switzerland, en route home from his Nepal trip, he learned that violence had erupted in the Republic of the Congo, immediately after it had gained its independence from Belgium. He hurried back to New York, ready for the Security Council meetings which were sure to follow.

Dag had long been worried about the situation in the Congo. It was one of the largest of the new African nations, and undoubtedly the richest in minerals. However, a UN representative said later, "It would be an understatement to say that no country was less prepared than the Congo to shoulder the responsibilities which came with independence. There were just eleven university graduates, not one Congolese doctor, judge, or magistrate, not one trained administrator, customs, or financial official, not a single engineer, or senior technician, and there was just one lawyer. It takes, however, at least two lawyers to argue a case—but there were no courts in which to try criminals . . ."

The Belgian Congo had been administered almost exclusively by Europeans. The governor-general, responsible only to the Belgian government, had had unrestricted power. Very few Congolese had positions of any responsibility whatever. Belgium had done a great deal to improve the living conditions and the health of the people in her large colony, but she had done little to prepare them for political independence.

On the promised date of freedom, June 20, 1960, King Baudouin of Belgium proclaimed the Congo independent, and the Belgian government moved out. However, Belgians were left behind in key positions which no Congolese had been trained to fill. Belgians remained as officers in the army and in the police force. They ran the communication and transportation facilities, and they operated all other public services.

With appropriate fanfare the Congolese took over the government of their own country. Joseph Kasavubu had been elected president, and Patrice Lumumba was made prime minister.

A few days after Independence Day, mutiny broke out in the army, the Force Publique. Congolese troops rebelled against their Belgian officers. Numerous incidents of violence followed throughout the new nation, including vicious attacks on Belgian civilians and their families. Large numbers of executives and technicians fled for their lives to Belgium or to the French Congo, across the river. Transportation and communication services were left without trained personnel. The main river port closed; the railroads shut down; airports had no technicians for their towers and radios, and they could not operate. The disappearance of doctors and nurses left the hospitals and health services unstaffed. Secondary schools closed for lack of teachers. Throughout the Congo many vital businesses and services came to a halt.

At once, without permission from the new Congolese government, Belgium sent troops into the Congo "to protect the lives and the property of Europeans there." Prime Minister Lumumba denounced this act as a gross violation of Congolese sovereignty.

Meanwhile other grave events threatened the very life of the new Congo nation. On July 11 Moise Tshombe, the pro-Belgian premier of Katanga Province, announced the secession of Katanga from the Congo. Tshombe wanted to see a federation of the Congo's provinces, in which the provinces had more power than the central government, while Lumumba believed in a strong federal government.

Katanga was the largest province in the Congo, and also the richest by far. Moneyed interests in Belgium feared that with a strong central government in the Congo, the rich mineral deposits of Katanga would slip out of their hands. So Tshombe had the backing of Belgian money and Belgian troops for his attempt to make Katanga a separate state with himself as its leader. It was logical to believe that Katanga would eventually play a leading role in the Congo federation that Tshombe visualized.

Lumumba opposed Tshombe bitterly. He rightly saw in the secession of Katanga the first step in dismemberment of the Republic of the Congo. The provinces of Kasai and Kivi were in danger of seceding too.

Prime Minister Lumumba appealed to the secretary-general of the United Nations for military aid against the Belgians. He also asked the UN to stop the secession of Katanga, accusing Belgium of plotting that secession in order to maintain a hold on the Congo.

On July 14, after an all-night session, the council passed a resolution calling on "the Government of Belgium to withdraw its troops from the Republic of the Congo." The council also authorized Dag "to provide the [Congo] Government with such military assistance as may be necessary . . ."

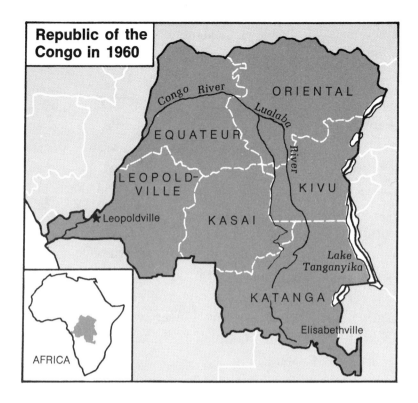

Republic of the Congo in 1960

Congo River

ORIENTAL

Lualaba

EQUATEUR

River

LEOPOLD-VILLE

KIVU

★ Leopoldville

KASAI

Lake Tanganyika

KATANGA

Elisabethville

AFRICA

The first UN troops landed in the Congo on July 15, and others followed a few days later. This second UN Emergency Force, known as ONUC (*Opération des Nations Unies au Congo*), soon numbered 3,500. There were 460 Ethiopians, 770 Ghanians, 1,250 Moroccans, and 1,020 Tunisians. Again the UN troops were instructed not to fight, but to prevent combat. They would fight only in self-defense. Within a few months the ONUC had increased to 20,000 troops.

Besides soldiers to keep order, the United Nations sent to the Congo a large number of professional workers, technicians, and administrators. These people

133

would help restore the public services that had been disrupted by the flight of Belgian experts.

Dag sent Ralph Bunche to the Congo as his special representative, to negotiate the withdrawal of Belgian forces. As ONUC soldiers began to arrive in the country, Belgian troops started to leave. But they did not withdraw fast enough to suit Prime Minister Lumumba and President Kasavubu. On July 17 the Congolese leaders sent an ultimatum to the United Nations. Unless all Belgian forces left the country within forty-eight hours, the Congo government would request aid from the Soviet Union, which had already expressed a willingness to send help.

Since the ultimatum posed impossible conditions, the appeal to the Soviet Union was soon made. In spite of a Security Council resolution that all aid to the Congo would be channeled through the United Nations, the Soviet Union sent Lumumba directly 100 military trucks, 29 transport planes, and 200 technicians. However, United Nations forces had taken charge of the Congo airports by then, and the Soviet aid was useless to Lumumba, at least temporarily.

Belgium had been particularly slow about withdrawing its troops from the seceding province of Katanga, claiming that the Belgians were needed there to maintain order. Dag insisted that the UN resolution of July 14 applied to Katanga as well as to the rest of the

Congo. Therefore, he wanted to send UN troops into Katanga to replace the Belgians, but Tshombe refused to allow any United Nations personnel in his territory, not even Ralph Bunche.

Dag then called Tshombe's attention to the principles that applied to the use of UN troops:

1. The troops were under the sole command and sole control of the United Nations.
2. They were not permitted to interfere in the internal affairs of the country where they were deployed.
3. They were not entitled to act except in self-defense.

Dag explained further that while the ONUC troops could not take the initiative in fighting, they were permitted "to reply by force to an armed attack."

After considerable negotiation, Hammarskjold finally secured Tshombe's permission to enter Katanga with a first detachment of ONUC troops. In Elisabethville, the capital of Katanga Province, Dag worked out an agreement with the Belgian commander, and within a week Belgian forces began to withdraw.

In going to Katanga Province with the ONUC, Dag had bypassed the Congo capital of Leopoldville. This infuriated Prime Minister Lumumba. He felt that he

UN soldiers (left) keep order in Leopoldville as the prime minister, Patrice Lumumba, holds a press conference.

should have been consulted. He wrote to Dag angrily, "You are acting as though my Government, which is the repository of legal authority and is alone qualified to deal with the United Nations, did not exist."

In his letters Lumumba referred to the UN Security Council resolution of July 14, which had authorized Dag "to provide the Government with such military assistance as may be necessary." He insisted that this resolution meant that UN troops should aid him in subduing the rebellious province of Katanga.

Dag was unable to make Lumumba understand that the UN forces were supranational troops, to be used only to prevent fighting. They could not be used for a purely political venture.

Lumumba wrote back furiously, "The Government and the people of the Congo have lost their confidence in the secretary-general of the United Nations." From that day on, Prime Minister Lumumba was a bitter enemy of Dag Hammarskjold.

At about this time Lumumba's plans for a strong central government for the Congo received another setback. Southern Kasai Province seceded, and bloody fighting and massacres followed. This was civil war. In addition, violence against the UN and its friends erupted all over the Congo. This violence was encouraged, if not incited, by Lumumba, who apparently intended to drive the United Nations troops out of the

Congo, since he could not use them as he wished. UN headquarters were raided, and UN personnel arrested. Crew members of a United States transport plane were beaten up. Canadian signalmen were attacked.

Then unbelievable events occurred in the Congo with bewildering speed. On September 5 President Kasavubu fired his prime minister, Patrice Lumumba. Lumumba then went on the radio and announced to the nation that Kasavubu was no longer chief of state. The Parliament, in a secret session, voted the power to Lumumba. Kasavubu claimed they did not have the authority to do this, and he suspended Parliament. On the same day the army seized control of the Congo government in a "peaceful revolution."

Parliament continued to support Lumumba, but the army threatened to arrest him, so he retired to his official residence on the bank of the Congo River.

The Congo was now broken up into four opposing factions. For eleven months the crisis continued. During this time there was really no legal government. The United Nations was in the unenviable position of trying to help a government, but not knowing which was the right government to help. As Ralph Bunche put it, the UN had "virtually the entire responsibility of holding things together in the Congo, while not trespassing on the authority of the government, when governmental machinery was just about nonexistent."

13. Mr. K Pounds His Desk

On September 20, 1960, the Fifteenth Session of the United Nations General Assembly opened, with sixteen new African nations scheduled to be admitted. It was a historic session, in more ways than one. During the first six weeks, thirty-four prime ministers and sixty-nine foreign ministers attended assembly meetings.

One after another, the representatives of various nations addressed the assembly. Nkrumah of Ghana, Sukarno of Indonesia, King Hussein of Jordan, Nasser of Egypt, Nehru of India, Macmillan of Great Britain, President Eisenhower of the United States, and many others made speeches. Castro of Cuba spoke for four and a half hours.

The star performer of the Fifteenth General Assembly Session was, without doubt, Nikita Khrushchev, head of the Soviet Union delegation and leader of the entire Soviet bloc of nations.

Dag, in the introduction to his annual report written a few weeks earlier, had called the United Nations the "main platform" and the "main protector" of new and weak nations. The Soviet Union, which hoped to extend its influence in Africa and Asia, did not share this concept of the UN. The Soviets disliked and feared the secretary-general's growing strength and popularity. They particularly objected to Dag's way of getting around a Soviet veto in the Security Council by referring the matter to the General Assembly, where the secretary-general could be sure of the necessary support.

On September 23 the Russian leader, Nikita Khrushchev, mounted the assembly rostrum. He put on his rimless eyeglasses and began to speak. For two hours he criticized the Western powers. He demanded "complete independence and freedom" for all colonial territories. He denounced the United Nations for its refusal to admit the People's Republic of China to membership. He accused the UN of gross mishandling of the Congo crisis. He called the United States an imperialist aggressor, and he demanded the immediate removal of United Nations headquarters from America, where, he said, blacks were treated as subhumans.

Then Khrushchev focused on the real purpose of his speech: criticism of Dag Hammarskjold. For an additional hour and a half, he leveled charge after charge at the secretary-general. He accused Dag of "siding with the colonialists" and of "misusing his power as secretary-general."

U. S. President Dwight D. Eisenhower addressed the
Fifteenth General Assembly Session of the United
Nations in September 1960.

The Soviet government, Khrushchev said, had now come to the conclusion that "the post of the secretary-general, who alone governs the staff and alone interprets and executes the decisions . . . should be abolished." The secretary-general should be replaced, Khrushchev declared, by a "collective executive body of three." This committee would represent "the military blocs of the Western powers, the Socialist States, and the Neutralist countries."

Amid cheers from the Soviet bloc delegates and grim silence from the Western representatives, the session adjourned for the weekend.

Over that weekend Khrushchev talked freely to newspaper and newsmagazine reporters. He made it very clear that his proposal was designed to give him a veto over all operations of the UN, not just those of the Security Council.

"All three members of the collective executive body must be agreed on a matter," he said. "They must be unanimous." He grinned at the reporters, and they understood clearly that Khrushchev would never allow any measure to pass that did not fit in with his own political plans.

On Monday morning, when the General Assembly opened, the atmosphere in the great hall was extremely tense. Everyone watched as Dag Hammarskjold made his way to his seat. All were wondering what he was thinking and feeling. How would he reply to the charges made by Khrushchev the previous week? Nothing could be guessed from Dag's calm, impassive face.

As soon as the meeting was opened, the secretary-general asked the chairman for permission to speak, and he was given the floor. In his usual unemotional, high-pitched voice, Dag began to reply to Khrushchev. He said that the matter before the assembly did not really concern the handling of the Congo problems, or any other action by the United Nations:

> . . . the General Assembly is facing a question . . . of the principles guiding United Nations' activities. In those respects it is a question not of a man but of an institution.

Dag talked about the principles that guided the United Nations and the secretary-general in their work in the Congo. Then he said:

> Sometimes one gets the impression that the Congo operation is looked at as being in the hands of the secretary-general, as somehow distinct from the United Nations. No: this is your operation, gentlemen. . . . It was the Security Council

which, without any dissenting vote, gave this mandate to the secretary-general on 14 July. It was the Security Council which, on 22 July, commended his report on the principles that should be applied. It was the Security Council, on 9 August, which, again without any dissenting vote, confirmed the authority given to the secretary-general. . . . Indeed, as I said, this is your operation, gentlemen. It is for you to indicate what you want to have done. . . . I am grateful for any positive advice, but if no such positive advice is forthcoming . . . then I have no choice but to follow my own conviction, guided by the principles to which I have just referred.

As Dag ended his speech, he was given a warm ovation, but Nikita Khrushchev pounded on his desk insolently. Gone was the geniality that Khrushchev had shown toward Dag Hammarskjold a year and a half earlier, in Russia. Throughout the remainder of the General Assembly session, Khrushchev heckled all the Western speakers, making as much noise as possible. Sometimes he banged on the table with both fists. Once, it is reported, he even took off his shoe and pounded his desk with that.

Premier Khrushchev (upper left) seated with his
delegation. His shoe can be seen on the desk.

On October 3 the Soviet leader again took the rostrum, and again he attacked Dag Hammarskjold. He
charged that the secretary-general had always been
prejudiced in his attitude toward the Socialist countries
and had always upheld the interests of the United
States "and the other monopoly-capitalist countries."

"In order to prevent any misinterpretation,"
Khrushchev went on, "I should like to repeat: We do
not and cannot place confidence in Mr. Hammarskjold.
If he himself does not muster up enough courage to

resign . . . then we shall draw the necessary conclu-sions."

When the session adjourned for lunch, Dag went up to the secretary-general's office on the thirty-eighth floor. He was soon joined by Cordier, Bunche, and Weischhoff. Dag was certain that Khrushchev was try-ing to pressure him into resigning, as the Soviets had done with Trygve Lie. Dag's assistants agreed with him.

When the General Assembly reconvened at 3:00 P.M., Dag was the first speaker. In the course of his speech, he said:

> I have no reason to defend myself or my colleagues against the accusations and judgments to which you have listened. Let me say only this, that *you*, all of you, are the judges. . . . I am sure you will be guided by truth and justice. . . .
>
> The man does not count. The institution does. A weak or nonexistent executive would mean that the United Nations would no longer be able to serve as an effective instrument. . . . The man hold-ing the responsibility as chief executive should leave if he weakens the executive; he should stay if this is necessary for its maintenance. . . .

. . . . By resigning, I would . . . at the present difficult and dangerous juncture throw the Organization to the winds. I have no right to do so. . . .

It is not the Soviet Union, or, indeed, any other big Powers who need the United Nations for their protection; it is all the others. In this sense the Organization is first of all *their* Organization, and I deeply believe in the wisdom with which they will be able to use it and guide it. I shall remain in my post . . .

As Dag spoke these words, he was interrupted by thunderous applause. Except for the delegates from the Soviet Union and its satellites, every representative in the immense hall was clapping and cheering wildly. Several minutes passed before Dag could finish his sentence:

I shall remain in my post during the term of my office as a servant of the Organization in the interests of all those other nations, as long as *they* wish me to do so.

When Dag finished his speech, the delegate from Tunisia rose to his feet. The delegate from the United

States followed. One by one, practically all members of the General Assembly, except those of the Soviet bloc, rose to give Dag Hammarskjold, secretary-general of the United Nations, a standing ovation.

To Nikita Khrushchev it must have been infuriating to see the representatives of all the new African nations on their feet, clapping and shouting to show their enthusiasm for Dag Hammarskjold. Khrushchev had undoubtedly counted on winning the support of those countries for himself. He had not succeeded in this, nor could he force Hammarskjold to resign.

14. The Road Ends

There was no peace yet in the Congo. With the army in power, with Lumumba disputing that power, with Kasavubu arguing with the Parliament, and with Tshombe still keeping Katanga Province separate from the Republic of the Congo, the result was practically anarchy. A UN representative described the situation like this:

"The Congo was like a ship adrift on mid-ocean, tossing about on the uneasy waters, abandoned by its crew, and full of panicky passengers."

To avoid arrest by the army, Patrice Lumumba refused to leave his home, the great mansion formerly occupied by the Belgian governor-general. Although he had tried to drive the UN out of the Congo, Lumumba now asked for UN protection. He got it in the form of a circle of ONUC guards around his house. But a ring of Congolese soldiers surrounded the UN guards. The situation was explained to Dag like this: "Mr. Lumumba is perfectly free to leave if he wants to, but the Congolese guard is there to prevent him from doing so. Our guard is to prevent unauthorized persons from coming in."

On December 20, 1960, Dag wrote to his friend Beskow, "I live in a kind of Congo inferno, where I have not a moment for myself." Indeed, for months he had been tied to his job, with little or no opportunity to escape either to his beloved Swedish farmhouse or to his Brewster hideaway. His chief comforts were the Meditation Room and poetry.

Dag had long since learned to find relaxation in poetry. When he became weary from wrestling with a certain type of intellectual problem, such as an international crisis, he found rest in using a different set of "mental muscles." His favorite field of mental exercise was poetry, especially the translation of poetry from one language to another. During the previous year, he

Dag searched endlessly for a solution to the problems of the Congo. The secretary-general is seen here boarding a plane at an airport in Katanga.

had translated into Swedish a book of French poetry, entitled *Chronique*, by Saint-John Perse. Later Perse won the Nobel Prize for Literature.

Besides reading and translating poetry, Dag found relaxation and pleasure in writing poems of his own. He began to compose *haiku*, that highly disciplined form of poetry in which he had long been interested. Some of his haiku concerned his childhood and his essential loneliness:

> *A box on the ear taught the boy*
> *That Father's name*
> *Was odious to them.*

> *   *   *

> *He fell when he tried to vault.*
> *They all had their laugh*
> *At such a sissy.*

> *   *   *

> *He wasn't wanted.*
> *When, nonetheless, he came,*
> *He could only watch them play.*

> *   *   *

> *School was over. The yard was empty.*
> *The ones he sought*
> *Had found new friends.*

Shortly before the end of 1960, Dag wrote a longer poem in his journal about what the future held in store for him:

> *The road,*
> *You shall follow it.*
>
> *The fun,*
> *You shall forget it.*
>
> *The cup,*
> *You shall empty it.*
>
> *The pain,*
> *You shall conceal it.*
>
> *The truth,*
> *You shall be told it.*
>
> *The end,*
> *You shall endure it.*

It was as if Dag Hammarskjold already knew what his end would be. From that time on, many entries in his journal concerned death and self-sacrifice for a cause.

Additional crises in the Congo kept Dag extremely busy. Patrice Lumumba had somehow escaped through the outer ring of Congolese soldiers which surrounded his home. Lumumba and three of his aides were finally captured by a unit of the Congolese army and returned to Leopoldville, bruised and bloody.

Kasavubu soon handed Lumumba over to Tshombe, his bitter enemy, who still maintained that Katanga was a separate nation. This action horrified United Nations personnel. Dag sent an immediate message to Tshombe urging humane treatment of the prisoner, pointing out the minimum rights generally accorded to an accused man. However, Tshombe replied, in effect, that his treatment of Lumumba was none of the UN's business, and he would not permit UN representatives even to visit the prisoner.

In January 1961 news leaked out that Lumumba had been murdered. At once he became a martyr to millions of Africans. Rioting erupted in many countries. Belgian embassies were attacked, and so were some American embassies. In protest against Lumumba's death, several African and Asian states withdrew their troops from the ONUC. These withdrawals gravely weakened the UN forces.

In the United Nations Security Council, Dag came under fire again from the Soviet Union.

"It is clear," the Soviet delegate said, "to every honest person throughout the world that the blood of Patrice Lumumba is on the hands of this henchman of the colonialists and cannot be removed. The Soviet government will not maintain any relations with Dag

Hammarskjold and will not recognize him as an official of the United Nations."

Obviously the Soviets were still trying to force the secretary-general to resign. However, Dag stayed at his post, as he had announced the previous autumn that he would. He set up a UN commission to investigate Lumumba's death, but it was denied entry into Katanga. The report of the commission said that Kasavubu and Tshombe "should not escape responsibility."

The long Fifteenth Session of the General Assembly ended in April, but the situation in the Congo remained as explosive as ever.

For many tense months, while trying to cope with one Congo crisis after another, the secretary-general had had little or no real rest. Even his exceptional health and stamina were not proof against such punishment. When Bo Beskow came to New York that spring to work on some murals for the UN library that Dag was planning, he found his friend changed. For the first time in their acquaintance Dag seemed truly tired, and very pessimistic—he who had always been, as he put it, a "blue-eyed optimist, believing in the possible."

On July 6 that summer of 1961, Dag wrote a poem in his diary, comparing his fatigue with that of a mountaineer midway in a dangerous climb:

Tired
And lonely,
So tired
The heart aches.
Meltwater trickles
Down the rocks,
The fingers are numb,
The knees tremble.
It is now,
Now, that you must not give in.

On the path of the others
Are resting places,
Places in the sun
Where they can meet.
But this
Is your path,
And it is now,
Now, that you must not fail.

Weep
If you can,
Weep,
But do not complain.
The way chose you—
And you must be thankful.

Dag's personal staff had worked long and faithfully during the entire period of the "Congo inferno." They called themselves the "Congo Club." Dag knew that he could not have endured these two years of heartbreaking strain without such loyal help.

Assistance to the Congo threatened to bankrupt the United Nations. It was costing ten million dollars a month to maintain the UN operation there, and no one knew how long it would be necessary to continue it. Fortunately the United States came to the rescue and offered to pay a large share of the costs.

In July 1961 the Parliament of the Republic of the Congo held its first formal session in nearly a year. A government was formed with Kasavubu as president and Cyrille Adoula as prime minister. Tshombe had promised to end the secession of Katanga and send delegates to the Parliament, but he did not keep his promises.

Within a month Tshombe was accusing the United Nations of planning to invade Katanga, and anti-UN demonstrations flared in Elisabethville, Katanga's capital. UN personnel were stoned, and a large-scale massacre was reportedly planned.

It was true that UN troops were planning to enter Katanga, but it was not meant to be a military attack.

Belgian troops had completed their official withdrawal from Katanga by September 1960. Unofficially,

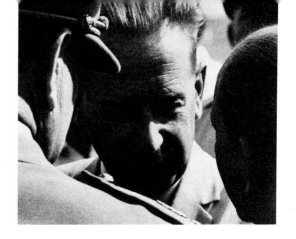

A troubled secretary-general (top) and two of the parties to the Congo dispute: Moise Tshombe of Katanga (middle) and Cyrille Adoula of the Republic of the Congo (bottom).

however, many foreign political advisers, military personnel, and mercenary soldiers remained, and more were entering the province all the time, apparently with Tshombe's blessing. By June 1961 there were more than 500 foreign mercenaries (hired soldiers) in the Katanga army, and the ONUC had been authorized by the Security Council to deport them. The central government of the Republic of the Congo had added its request to that of the Security Council for this action, and the ONUC troops began to round up all foreigners in Katanga for deportation. Tshombe had promised to cooperate, but he did not. About half of the mercenaries could not be found for deportation, and UN personnel believed that Tshombe was purposely hiding them. The project was less than a success.

Early in September Dag received an invitation from Prime Minister Adoula of the Republic of the Congo to visit Leopoldville, to discuss United Nations' "aid and support" to the central government.

Dag welcomed this invitation. He would fly to the Congo as soon as possible and see what he could accomplish with personal diplomacy. There was no time to lose, for he must be back in New York by September 19, when the Sixteenth Session of the General Assembly was due to open. Dag was determined that, while in the Congo, he would talk to Tshombe in person, regardless of the dangers of such a meeting. He would do his utmost to persuade Tshombe to cooperate with the government of the Republic of the Congo and with the United Nations.

On September 8, UN Staff Day, Dag made a speech to the 4,000 UN employees. In part, he said:

Those who serve the Organization can take pride in what it has already done in many, many cases. I know what I am talking about if I say, for example, that short of the heavy work in which each of you has had his or her part, the Congo would by now have been torn to pieces in a fight which in all likelihood would not have been limited to that territory, but spread far around, involving directly or indirectly many or all of the countries from which you come . . .

When Dag finished his speech, he received a tremendous ovation. There was no doubt about the warm feelings of the UN staff toward the secretary-general.

Two days later, as was his custom before leaving on a trip, Dag visited the Meditation Room for a period of outer silence and inner stillness.

As he left the Secretariat building that evening, a UNICEF official, Grace Barbey, stopped him.

"Mr. Secretary-General," she said, "you are going on a mission of great importance. You must know that we in the Secretariat are behind you all the way."

"Yes," Dag replied. "I do know, and it is one of the strengths I carry with me."

Grace Barbey turned to Bill Ranallo, who stood beside the car at the curb, waiting for the secretary-general. "Bill, take good care of him," she begged.

"I sure will," Bill Ranallo answered, and Dag Hammarskjold smiled. No one really knew how well Bill took care of him, how dedicated he was to the protection and the welfare of his charge. No man ever had a more faithful friend and aide than Bill Ranallo.

The following day Dag and Bill Ranallo boarded a plane for the Congo. Several members of the "Congo Club" were there to see Dag off. They did not know that they were making their final farewells to the secretary-general.

15. "A Clear Pure Note"

As the chartered jet plane flew high over the Atlantic, Dag quietly read the book he had brought with him, Thomas à Kempis' *Imitation of Christ*. His bookmark was imprinted with the oath of office he had taken on his accession to the secretary-general post: "I, Dag Hammarskjold, solemnly swear to exercise in all loyalty, discretion, and conscience the functions entrusted to me as secretary-general of the United Nations . . ."

On September 13, while Dag and his party were still in flight, the Congo situation worsened drastically. Tshombe's Congolese soldiers, led by white officers and with many foreign mercenaries in their ranks, attacked an Irish company of the ONUC. At the same time fighting broke out in Elisabethville, Katanga's capital. It was now full-scale war against UN troops by Tshombe's men and foreign mercenaries.

The attacks of the white mercenaries were even more vicious than those of the blacks. A jet plane, a Fouga, was particularly destructive. Whenever the pilot saw a spot of blue (ONUC troops wore blue helmets and carried the blue and white UN flag), he dropped a bomb on it.

When Dag Hammarskjold landed in Leopoldville, capital of the Republic of the Congo, he heard the appalling news of the fighting. At once he instructed his Congo representative, Conor O'Brien, to negotiate a cease-fire with Tshombe, but this proved to be a very difficult assignment. Tshombe hid away, thus foiling UN attempts at negotiation.

The situation infuriated Dag Hammarskjold. He had come to the Congo to prove to the world his firm conviction that international conflicts could be resolved by means of persuasion and conciliation. But how could you persuade a man when you couldn't talk to him? Dag feared that a personal failure in Katanga would mean a failure of the United Nations itself, a drastic lowering of its prestige around the world. That prospect did not bear thinking about.

Four days passed. Tshombe was not to be found. The date for the meeting of the General Assembly—the deadline for Dag's return to New York—was fast approaching. Still he had made no progress in the Congo situation.

At midnight on the fourth day, September 16, Dag received word that Tshombe would meet a UN representative in Ndola, Northern Rhodesia. Dag replied at once, requesting an immediate cease-fire. He went on:

I suggest that I should try to meet you personally so that together we can try to find peaceful methods of resolving the present conflict, thus opening the way to a resolution of the Katanga problem within the framework of the Congo.

Tshombe answered with a conditional acceptance of Dag's cease-fire. He demanded that UN troops be immobilized, while his own soldiers were left free to kill. Dag could not accept these terms. He called for an unconditional cease-fire.

Dag received no reply from Tshombe to this last message. He was told that Tshombe was already planning to go to Ndola to meet him, so he prepared to fly to the rendezvous.

Ordinarily the secretary-general flew in United Nations airplanes. This time, for some reason known only to himself, Dag Hammarskjold decided not to. Unaccountably he chose a commercial plane, called the *Albertina,* a DC-6 belonging to a Swedish company. This plane was usually used by the commander of UN troops and had been fired on a few days earlier by foreign mercenaries. It had suffered considerable damage.

By 4 P.M. on Sunday, September 17, the damage to the *Albertina* had been repaired, and Dag and his party could prepare for departure.

Before the secretary-general was allowed to board the airplane, Bill Ranallo and a fellow security officer made a routine but thorough check of the plane. They found nothing suspicious, and Dag was ushered aboard. He carried his briefcase, which contained the papers and documents he needed for the meeting with Tshombe. It also held an extra shirt, a toothbrush, and a book he was translating into Swedish. Nine aides followed Dag, including security officer Sergeant Harold Julien, four guards from the ONUC, and of course Bill Ranallo.

Dag had been urged by his staff not to make this trip at this time and in this way. Diplomats of various countries then in the Congo capital had warned against it. There had been too much violence against UN personnel in Katanga for anyone connected with the world organization to be safe. Moreover, a night flight would be extremely dangerous in this strife-torn country. The sole advantage of leaving Leopoldville so late in the afternoon would lie in the fact that darkness would hamper an attack by the vicious pilot of the Fouga jet plane.

Strangely, Dag would listen to no warnings. Apparently he was so intent on the importance of meeting with Tshombe personally that he closed his eyes to the perils surrounding the trip.

As if the proposed flight were not sufficiently hazardous at best, several normal precautions were flouted. The *Albertina*'s flight plan was kept secret, and the pilot was under instructions to maintain radio silence.

In a newspaper interview shortly before embarking, Dag stressed the necessity of driving foreign mercenaries out of Katanga. The UN action was being sabotaged, he said, by Belgians, South Africans, Rhodesians, and above all French adventurers, "the dregs and refuse from Algiers."

The *Albertina* took off from the Leopoldville airport about 5 P.M. on September 17, and that was the last that the United Nations staff in the Congo knew of the flight.

Six hours later, at 10 P.M. at Ndola airport, the *Albertina* was seen coming in as if preparing to land. The pilot broke radio silence at last and announced that he was descending. Instructions were immediately sent from the Ndola radio tower for the landing.

The *Albertina* circled the field, apparently making the turn preparatory to coming down. Then it disappeared into the darkness. What happened after that will probably never be known.

In Uppsala: Dag's coffin is escorted through the ancient university town by white-capped students. At the United Nations: The UN flag is flown at half-mast for the fallen secretary-general.

At one o'clock the following afternoon, the smoldering wreck of the *Albertina* was found in the jungle nine miles from the Ndola airport. All but two of the passengers had died in the burning plane. Dag Hammarskjold and Sergeant Julien had been thrown clear of the wreckage.

Dag was dead when the plane was discovered, but Julien, although gravely injured, was still alive. He could give no coherent account of the tragedy, however. At the last minute before the expected landing, he said, Dag had given an order to the pilot to turn back. Before he could say anymore, Julien died.

That is all that is known for sure about Dag Hammarskjold's last flight. The rest is speculation.

UN representative Conor O'Brien later wrote, "In Elisabethville, I do not think there was anyone who believed that his death was an accident." Another UN official said, "A lot has not been told."

The fact remains that Dag Hammarskjold was dead. However, two days later Tshombe signed the cease-fire that Dag had been working for, and Congo unity was possible at last.

The bodies of the victims of the crash were flown back to their homelands. At each place where the plane that carried them touched down, crowds gathered to pay their respects to the memory of the late, great secretary-general of the United Nations.

When the plane reached Sweden, all the flags were flying at half-mast to mourn Dag Hammarskjold and the Swedish crew members who had died with him. Statesmen from all over the world assembled at the cathedral in Uppsala for the funeral. At the right of the flag-draped coffin sat the king and queen of Sweden, and at the left were Dag's brothers, Bo and Sten, with their families.

After the service an open gun carriage drawn by four horses (which had previously been used only for royal funerals) bore the coffin through the narrow streets to the family grave in the peaceful cemetery near the university. Uppsala University students, wearing the traditional white cap and the uniform that Dag had worn for years, lined the streets. Walking behind the Hammarskjold family in the long procession were people of every race and every faith.

The question that Dag had written as the first entry in his diary, thirty-one years earlier, had been answered:

Shall I ever get there?
There where life resounds,
A clear pure note
In the silence.

The entire free world now realized that Dag

Hammarskjold's life had indeed been "a clear pure note."

John F. Kennedy, president of the United States, said of Dag, "His name will occupy a prominent place among the peacemakers of history."

Emperor Haile Selassie of Ethiopia said, "He sacrificed himself for the cause . . . that war should end and peace prevail."

An American journalist had once called Dag Hammarskjold the "world's greatest natural asset." The world now recognized that he had made of the secretary-general's office an effective instrument for peace. He had done much to prove that negotiation and arbitration could make progress toward the chief aim of the United Nations, as stated in the Charter:

. . . To save succeeding generations from the scourge of war . . .

Dag Hammarskjold had given his life for peace. With his death the United Nations faced a vital question: Would his work be nullified in succeeding years, or would it be carried on by others for the eventual triumph that Dag Hammarskjold had hoped for—"Peace on earth, goodwill toward men"?

Chronological List of Events in Dag Hammarskjold's Life

1905 Dag Hjalmar Agne Carl Hammarskjold is born on July 29 in Jonkoping, Sweden.

1907 His father is appointed lord lieutenant of Uppland Province. The ancient castle in Uppsala becomes the family home.

1930 Shortly after receiving his law degree from the University of Uppsala, Dag moves to Stockholm and is made secretary of the Royal Commission on Unemployment.

1933 Dag receives his doctorate on the basis of the report he has written for the Royal Commission on Unemployment. During the early part of the 1930s, he becomes secretary of the Bank of Sweden and then the principal clerk of the Finance Ministry. He serves in the last two positions simultaneously for a time.

1936 Dag is appointed undersecretary of the Finance Ministry, the youngest man ever to hold the post.

1946 Dag becomes a special adviser to the Foreign Ministry. Several years later he is appointed secretary-general of this ministry.

1951 He is made vice-minister of foreign affairs and as such, a member of the Swedish cabinet.

1953 On April 7, Dag Hammarskjold's nomination as secretary-general of the United Nations is confirmed by the General Assembly. He arrives in New York on April 9 to accept the appointment.

1954 In December, the General Assembly passes a resolution instructing Hammarskjold to obtain the release of American airmen held prisoner in China.

1955 In January he visits Peking, and six months later the American airmen are released.

1956 Following a round-the-world trip, he is requested by the Security Council in March to return to the Middle East because of a breakdown of the 1949 Arab-Israeli Armistice Agreements. By May he has brought about a cease-fire. In July Egypt nationalizes the Suez Canal. On October 29, Israeli troops invade Egyptian territory. France and Great Britain take military action in the area. On November 7, the General Assembly accepts Hammarskjold's plan for the formation of a UN Emergency Force to be sent to the Middle East to maintain a cease-fire.

1957 Dag Hammarskjold is reelected secretary-general of the United Nations.

1958 Employing the philosophy of "UN Presence," Hammarskjold settles disputes such as those between Cambodia and Thailand, Lebanon and the United Arab Republic, and others.

1959   In March he undertakes an inspection tour of possible trouble areas in Asia. He visits Russia as the guest of Premier Nikita Khrushchev.

1960   Dag travels through Africa during the early part of this year. Calling this "The Year of Africa," he makes plans for raising funds to help the new nations. The Congo crisis develops in July, and the first UN troops land in the Congo on July 15. Hammarskjold visits Elisabethville and Leopoldville. In September at the Fifteenth General Assembly Session, Khrushchev seeks the dismissal of Hammarskjold.

1961   The Soviet Union again tries to force the resignation of Hammarskjold. Full-scale war breaks out against UN forces in the Congo on September 13. Determined to negotiate a cease-fire, Hammarskjold flies from Leopoldville on Sunday, September 17, for a meeting at Ndola on the Rhodesian border. The plane crashes, and the following day the body of Dag Hammarskjold is found near the wreckage. He is buried at Uppsala, Sweden.

Index

Picture credits:

Karsh, Ottawa: cover and jacket
The New York Times: p. 145
Lennart Nilsson from Black Star: p. 83
Pressens Bild from Photoreporters, Inc.: p. 36
Reportagebild, Stockholm: p. 166 (top)
Swedish Information Service: pp. 15, 20, 24, 29, 42, 58, 67, 89
Swedish Touring Club: p. 46
United Nations: pp. 53, 72, 77, 80, 94, 102, 119, 136 (top), 141, 150, 157 (all)
United Press International: pp. 110 (both), 124, 136 (bottom)
Wide World Photos, Inc.: p. 166 (bottom)